50 Ideas to Boost Your Writing

Steve Bowkett

© NAWG Publications 2005

Published by NAWG Publications, 2005

Copyright © Steve Bowkett, 2005

ISBN 0-9546461-4-2

The right of Steve Bowkett to be identified
as the author of this work has been asserted
by him in accordance with the Copyright,
Designs and Patents Act 1988

A catalogue for this book is
available from the British Library

First published in Great Britain by
NAWG Publications, The Arts Centre
Biddick Lane, Washington, Tyne & Wear NE38 2AB

Printed and bound in Great Britain by
Jasprint Ltd., Tyne & Wear

Acknowledgements

I wish to thank the Board of Trustees of NAWG and NAWG's Editorial Committee for being so supportive of this project. Their enthusiasm for the book, and for writing generally, has made and continues to make working with them a pleasure. They are good companions along the writer's long and sometimes lonely road.

I owe a large debt of gratitude (and certainly a bottle with the word malt on the label) to Brian Lister who cast a 'friendly critical' eye over the manuscript. His perceptive, wise and practical advice has been invaluable.

I'm also very grateful to Mike Wilson, NAWG's workhorse (and warhorse!) whose inexhaustible energies I envy, and whose expertise has allowed '50 Ideas' to become a reality.

The ideas and techniques in this book have developed over many years through using them in schools, with writers' groups and in other contexts. I acknowledge the help (intentional or otherwise) of all these good people here.

My friend Douglas Hill deserves a special mention. We have on many occasions met and talked about the world and the craft of writing. Doug has been a great mentor and I treasure his wisdom.

Thanks also to my friends Russell Morgan for artwork on pages 18 and 68, and Chris Pepper for artwork on pages 32 and 92.

Finally - and never least - I thank my wife Wendy and dedicate this book to her. She lets me sit and write every day. What a perfect mate!

"To remain a pupil is to serve your teacher badly." - Nietzche

Contents

		Page
	Introduction	9
1.	Link to Think - generating ideas by choosing random pictures	11
2.	Propp's Magic Formula - basic narrative elements	15
3.	Many Viewpoints - visualising different perspectives	17
4.	Consult the Oracle - using a coin to generate answers to yes/no questions	19
5.	Storyline It - a visual plotting technique	21
6.	Sleep On It - exploiting the subconscious mind	24
7.	Anchors and Filters - training useful behaviours in writing	27
8.	Six Big Important Questions - questioning techniques for generating ideas	30
9.	Picture It - engaging the senses	33
10.	Visualising - visualising as a creative tool	36
11.	Bottom-Up-Top-Down Storymaking - organising a story	38
12.	Creating Contexts - using vague sentences to learn more about a story	45
13.	Creating Convincing Characters - some hints and tips	49
14.	Top-Down-Bottom-Up-Characters - organising information about characters	56
15.	Back to the Starting Grid - using images to deepen understanding of characters	59
16.	Bundles of Contradictions - character profiling	62
17.	It's All in the Mind - jumping into your characters' shoes	66

18.	A Sense of Place - evoking the uniqueness of settings	70
19.	Focus of Attention - using the imagination as a mental 'zoom tool' for narrative perspectives	73
20.	Jigsaw Town - inventing locations	78
21.	The Colour of Saying - cross-matching senses to develop originality	80
22.	Emotional Impact - evoking feelings in your readers	83
23.	Stuff and Nonsense - developing a sense of words	86
24.	Practice Piece 1 - The Walker - some revision!	91
25.	Collecting Motifs - exploring details of genre	94
26.	Position Statements and Fortune Cookie Language - creating details out of vague statements	96
27.	The Ten Sentence Game - exploring and expanding plots	98
28.	The Merlin Game - brainstorming variations on your ideas	100
29.	Dear Diary - using diaries to develop stories and overcome writer's block	102
30.	Till Roll Writing - a technique for stream-of-consciousness writing	104
31.	Story Tree - making the most of a plot idea	106
32.	How Do They Do It? - studying other authors	108
33.	Thumbnails - keeping track of characters, settings and plot ideas	110
34.	Blurb It - picking out your story's individuality	112
35.	Be Somebody (Else) - the usefulness of pseudonyms	113
36.	The Journeyman - appraising your attitude to writing	116
37.	Countdown to a Story - a checklist as you prepare to write or review	118

38.	A Sense of Audience - focusing on your readers	121
39.	Casting a Critical Eye - general reviewing of your work	125
40.	The Soul of Style - learn the rules well and then forget them - the flow of composition	128
41.	Practice Piece 2: Going Along for the Ride - some more revision	130
42.	Into the Wild Blue Yonder - tips for submitting your work	138
43.	Agents and Etiquette - pros and cons of seeking agents	141
44.	Nightmare Tales - be prepared for rejections, and worse!	143
45.	Vanity, Thy Name is Publishing - tips and opinions on self-publishing your work	147
46.	So, What's Your Attitude? - tips for staying positive	151
47.	Wishes, Goals, Pledges and Dares - taking control of your feelings	152
48.	The Road to Mastery - maintaining a sense of positive purpose	153
49.	Every Day Parables - writing down your wisdom	155
50.	CREATE - summing up	159
Index		161

"When someone points to the moon, the fool looks at the finger and the wise person looks at the moon."

Introduction

The famous Science Fiction writer Arthur C. Clarke once said that a lack of progress in science comes from a failure of imagination or a failure of nerve. The same might be said of writing. A failure of imagination manifests itself in ways such as 'How can I write the book that I know is inside me?' 'How can I get my characters out of this situation?' 'How can I think of a title for my story?' or even 'How can I turn all these feelings and images in my head into words on the page?'

A failure of nerve shows itself in ways such as 'I'll never be able to start/finish this project!' 'I can't send this off, it's hopeless!' 'I might as well give up, so-and-so is much better than I am!' 'But what if people hate it?' 'I'm bound to get rejected!'

These are real concerns and no-one (least of all myself) denies that they have a great effect on any writer's development. However, the first and perhaps most important point I want to make in this book is that failures of imagination and nerve exist inside of us. They are our own personal responses to perceived fears, lack of capability, or whatever. *And this is good news,* because there are ways of gaining more control of and changing what goes on within us in terms of our thoughts, feelings and behaviours.

And this is what *50 Ideas to Boost Your Writing* is all about.

Perhaps I should say a little bit about what qualifies me to talk to you about what goes on inside your own mind and your own heart. Well, I've experienced the same things. I was grabbed by the writing bug at that most vulnerable of times in one's life, when I was just entering adolescence. I had little self-esteem and virtually no confidence. Writing was a way of escaping from the big bad world and doing in imagination all the things I really wanted to do in life, but was too frightened to attempt or believed were not possible.

My learning-by-trial-and-error carried on through my teens and into my adult life as a teacher of English. By then I was attempting novels as well as writing short stories and poems, mainly for therapy, and because I had a certain hunger inside to do something special with my life. If you aim to write, or are already doing it, I'm sure you'll recognise that feeling. By age 25 I began systematically submitting a handful of novels I'd written - and just as systematically collecting a pile of rejections that ranged from detailed analyses of what was wrong with my work to blank compliments slips returned with the (clearly unread) manuscript.

Was I angry? Was I hurt? Of course I was. But by then I was developing 'The Attitude.' which has sustained me ever since. Such an attitude is made up of things like -

- Determination
- faith in one's own ability to write and complete the work
- looking to future projects with a sense of excited anticipation
- realising that, whatever the fate of my story or poem, my achievement lies in having written it
- understanding that editors, agents and the like are just people with opinions. Their judgements can be wrong
- treasuring and valuing the ideas that one's own mind produces
- accepting that if there's a problem with the work, I can write my way out of it.

The Attitude has more to it than this, of course. It is a complex, subtle, dynamic energy that drives the writing forward. What I want to do in this book is to show you some of the tools, tips and techniques that I have developed to translate that frame of mind into written output.

My good friend, the writer Douglas Hill, was once asked by a child 'Why do you write?' Doug's reply was, 'Son, why do you breathe?'

Let's proceed on that assumption.

Steve Bowkett
www.sbowkett.freeserve.co.uk

1

50 Ideas to Boost Your Writing

Link to Think

> *The work shows you how to do it.*
> *Traditional Estonian proverb*

We cannot help but put bits of information together to create bigger ideas. An idea is a 'mental form,' and we are all pretty good at making up these structures. In fact we do it naturally. Consciously we are aware of 'trains of thought' - lines of ideas that fit logically together. The subconscious part of the mind, the dreaming realm that seethes with creativity, weaves *networks* of ideas all the time, that constantly feed back into the vast and complex 'map of reality' that lies inside our heads. One way of generating more raw material for writing is to tap into this incredible networking engine that is the subconscious realm.

Look at **Fig.1** on the following page. Here we have thirty-six little pictures. Some of them are immediately recognisable, while some of them may seem ambiguous and puzzling. How do you feel about not knowing what some of these images might be? A healthy approach is to decide to feel comfortable in this situation. If you're happy not to know the 'right answer' just yet, that keeps the doorway open to explore many possibilities later.

We will locate items on the grid by going 'along the corridor and up the stairs.' In other words, we count along the bottom, beneath the first row, and then count upwards. So 3/4 corresponds to the image of the bird, 5/2 leads us to the castle and so on.

Prove to yourself that your mind can pop up ideas quickly and easily. Use a dice (I never say 'die') to select images at random. Put

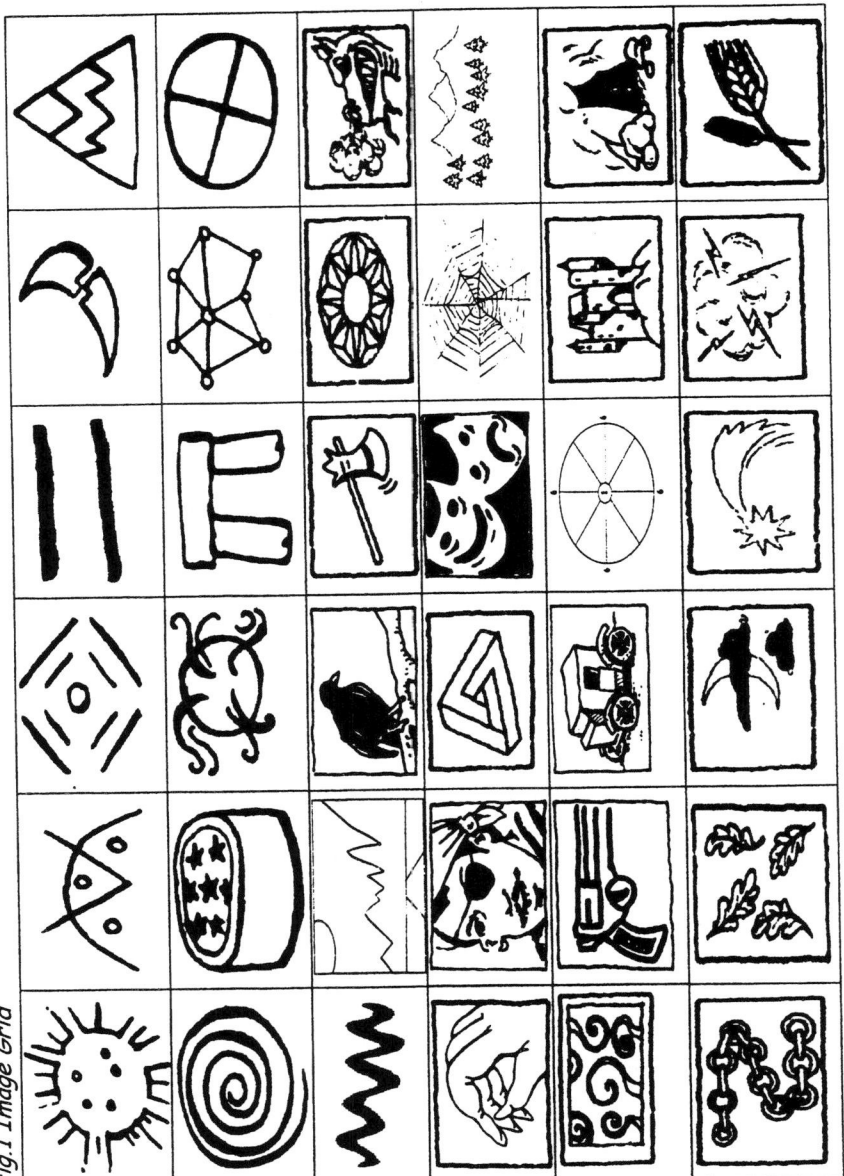

Fig.1 Image Grid

yourself in a calm, relaxed state. Expect only that you'll have good ideas very soon. There's no need to try to work anything out.

Roll the dice twice to pick one image. Now pick a second image and let your mind link them together. Notice the first impression that comes along. It might be a simple, literal link or a broader, more metaphorical impression. In any event, scribble down your idea. I just rolled 2/6 and 5/3. What occurred to me was that the spider-web represented the networks of ideas I've just been talking about, while the 'pair of compasses' icon suggested going outside the circle into fresh fields, but keeping the focus or centre safe.

What does this mean precisely? I don't know yet - but I feel comfortable with not knowing the answer(s) right now. I'm content to let the notion simmer in the back of my mind and to let further insights come along later. And for me that's the essence of creative thinking.

But what if the vague notions I've picked off the grid don't turn into something clearer? If you doubt yourself in this way you are denying the power of your own imagination. A vital aspect of boosting creative ability is to maintain a *clear intent* that things will happen and turn out well. Intent is active and positive. (Hope, by the way, is on the other hand passive, static and can be riddled with uncertainty.) I *intend* to have clear ideas, and by telling myself so I am constantly instructing my brain to do its work effectively.

You can create this kind of focus immediately. Let's go back to our grid and consider the first scene of a story (it doesn't matter if this story doesn't yet exist). Roll the dice twice to select one item off the grid. Anticipate that wherever you land you'll find out something about how the story will start . . .

I rolled 1/3 and landed on the rather sinister-looking long-nailed hand. That very image would make for a great opening paragraph.

How would the rest of that scene unfold? I don't know yet, but I could use the grid to guide me further (see below), or just let that opening image simmer in my mind and wait for more ideas to come - as I know they will.

A little trick that helps the imagination to do its work is found in the phrase 'whatever the dice selects will tell us *something about . . .*' That instruction is 'artfully vague,' which means that we are giving the brain a definite task - we *will* be told something - but the outcome is uncertain at the moment. There are endless possibilities as to what it might be. Remember that these techniques are most effective when you are not trying hard to figure out ideas. We are not working primarily with the conscious, analytical part of the mind at this point.

But now for some further focus. You can construct a sequence of events for a possible story by playing the zig-zag-story game. Return to the grid and locate yourself at the bottom left-hand corner. Roll the dice *once* so that you pick an item along the bottom row. Tell yourself that wherever you land you will find out something about how the story starts (scribble down your insights). Roll the dice again; this might take you around the corner on to the second row. Wherever you land will tell you something about what happens next. From here continue making dice rolls that move up the grid snakes-and-ladders style. Wherever you land you will be told something about the next bit of your story. Along the top row, as you choose a final image or two, you will be told something about how your story could end.

You now have a sequence of events more or less clearly arranged. If something in the sequence doesn't make enough sense, *go back to the resource*: roll the dice twice and wherever you land you will have an insight into how to make any area of confusion clearer.

We'll be returning to our ideas grid from time to time through the book, but for now let's add some more tools to our workbox.

2

50 Ideas to Boost Your Writing

Propp's Magic Formula - basic narrative elements

> What lies behind us and what lies ahead of us are small matters compared to what lies within us.
> *Ralph Waldo Emerson*

Some time back a folklorist named Vladimir Propp wondered why broadly similar stories had evolved independently in different cultures across the world. He was also intrigued as to why some stories made such an impact that they were handed down generation after generation. Propp compared thousands of folk tales from across the world and discovered that at the heart of all powerful stories there exists a cluster of basic structural elements. These are:

* A **Hero** or heroine representing noble qualities and struggling on the side of good.
* A **Villain** or villainess opposing the hero. The villain creates a
* **Problem** that forms the core of the story, and which the hero must resolve. To do this the hero may require
* A **Partner**, as indeed may the villain. This arrangement immediately creates the opportunity for dialogue and scene-hopping as characters separate. In order for the hero to resolve the problem, and in order that the villain may prevent this, both character archetypes will need
* **Help**. This may come in the form of a further character, natural circumstances, magic, etc. The dynamic of the story is accelerated by the inclusion of

* **Knowledge and power.** This often takes the form of one character or group gaining the advantage over another. The story is moved on by knowledge and power of various kinds 'changing hands,' as it were, throughout the narrative. Such power may be embodied in a significant
* **Object.** Again this may take the form of a living being. It is also frequently tied into the central problem of the story very deeply.

If you think about your own favourite book, film or TV series, you may well be able to identify most or all of these elements. Remember though that these create the basic structure of a narrative: overlying this 'girderwork' are further layers and refinements, which make up the rich embroidery of a story. We will look at these presently.

Many Viewpoints

> To know someone well, walk a mile in his shoes.
> *Traditional saying*

The ability to look at things from a range of perspectives is a valuable skill in developing one's writing. It really comes down to mental flexibility. Perhaps most obviously we can assume the author's 'godlike' narrative viewpoint as we look down upon the whole world of the story, and see it from the perspective of any or all of our characters. The writer Anais Nin made the point that we see the world not as it is, but as we are, so that if we can appreciate someone else's feelings, then we develop the quality of empathy and are already beginning to look at the world as they are doing. Empathy of course requires that we actively seek to *understand* another person's viewpoint: simply to weep as someone else weeps is, strictly speaking, sympathy, which involves feelings but not necessarily the leap of imagination into the other person's world that I am talking about.

We can take the notion of 'many viewpoints' further. If you have an idea for a novel, perhaps some of its constituent ideas would also work as a short story, or a play, or perhaps its themes could generate poetry? When you next pass judgement on someone (the driver who's just cut you up is a perfect example!), take a few moments to consider why he did that. Maybe he really is a poor driver. Maybe he's a businessman who's late for an important meeting. Maybe his wife is ill in hospital and he's rushing to be by her side . . . If you have the presence of mind to think like this, firstly you have more control over which option you choose to believe and therefore over the feelings that make up your response. This is

Fig.2: Family?

what responsibility amounts to - the ability we have to respond. Secondly, by gaining more conscious control over the ways in which you look at that person or situation, you can play about with that range of perspectives and create in your imagination many windows through which to look at the world.

Treat yourself and play the *I Wonder Game*. Consider the sentence below in conjunction with **Fig.2**.

They shook hands, but only Baxter was smiling.

Let me say that intriguing, question-begging sentences like this are a great way of getting the creative juices flowing, and we'll be coming back to them later. For now, use the sentence and the picture of these characters together and make a list of 'I wonders,' with a special emphasis on what these people may be feeling, and why, and what they might do about it. In other words, weave the sentence above into their story and think about how the world looks to them.

4

50 Ideas to Boost Your Writing

Consult the Oracle

> Include the knower in the known.
> *Traditional Wisdom*

Although I want to offer you plenty of resources in this book to boost your writing, the true resource really is your own mind and imagination. It truly is a 're-source,' you source it again and again to give you the help that you need.

Look again at **Fig.1** (the little picture grid) and have a dice ready. Prepare to roll the dice twice and say to yourself, 'whatever the dice picks out will tell me something about Baxter.' The dice will select the image - then simply notice the idea(s) that pop into your head. You can use the same technique to find out *something about* the hero in a story, the villain, the problem - right down to the end of Propp's list.

Here's a tip. If the dice selects a picture and you find yourself struggling to figure out what it means, stop struggling and roll the dice twice more. Wherever you land that will give you a clue as to how to use the first picture to answer your question. Go back to the resource.

Heads or Tails? This is another technique I use to generate information quickly and easily. Take a coin and ask a yes-no (closed) question about our sentence 'They shook hands but only Baxter was smiling.' So you might ask 'Is Baxter a man?' Flip the coin. Heads gives a *yes* answer and tails gives a *no* answer. You now have an easy way of systematically asking closed questions to learn more about the plot, characters and background of your work in progress.

Using the coin technique might not of course give you the answers you want, or those that are most useful. Instead of arguing with the coin, continue to accumulate information. When you have plenty of raw material, look back over it and ask, 'What do I need to discard, what shall I keep, what shall I change?' You are, after all, the rider of that powerful horse which is your imagination.

5

50 Ideas to Boost Your Writing

Storyline It

> New and stirring things are often belittled,
> because if they were not, the humiliating question arises
> - why then are you not taking part in them?
> *H. G. Wells*

At school we learn that a story has a beginning, a middle and an end*. Such stories unfold in a long line of words or sounds and images. Although subconsciously our mind explores narratives holistically (which is why ideas from any part of the story can pop up apparently at random), the time comes when we need to put that wonderful array of ideas into a sequence - and further organise them when we compose our stories word by word.

(* I once visited a school to talk about my books and mentioned that a story consisted basically of three parts. A little boy put his hand up and said, 'I know Stephen, a beginning, a muddle and an end.' I knew exactly what he meant).

This broad sequencing of ideas can sometimes be a struggle. We may feel swamped with too much imagery or detail, or we may not know right then how our ideas can fit together. And what if other ideas come along later (as they probably will), how can they be accommodated?

A good technique to use here is a story line. Take a *large* sheet of paper and draw a horizontal line right across it midway down the sheet. On the left put 'B.' In the centre of the line put 'M.' At the right of the line put ... You've guessed it. You can now annotate the line, marking in the positions of important incidents. If you have an

Fig.3 - Story Line

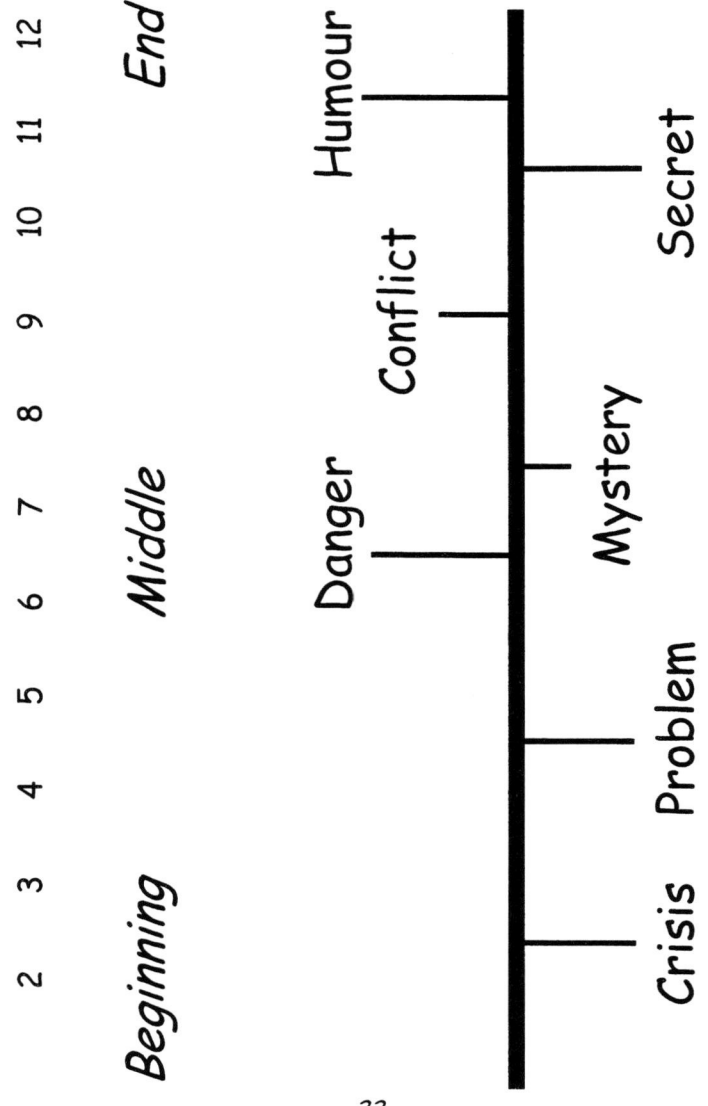

idea that fits towards the end of the story, make a short note at that point along the line. In this way you will build up a highly organised sequence of ideas that you can review at a glance. Both your 'big picture' subconscious and your logical-linear conscious mind will feel satisfied.

The basic storyline idea can be used in other ways. Refer to **Fig.3**. Here we have marked rather vague 'ingredients' such as danger or conflict. What do they mean? Well, you can use the dice and 6x6 grid to find out more, or systematically ask questions using coin flips to find out more.

The number line along the top of the diagram allows you to roll two dice at once. You'll get a number between 2 and 12. 'Drop into' the story at that point and use the techniques above to explore further.

6

Sleep On It

> It is an ancient story,
> yet it is ever new.
> *Heinrich Heine*

Sometimes people ask me about the book I'm working on right now. I always reply truthfully that I'm working on *several* books right now, although I don't always know that I'm doing it. The fact is that there is a lot more going on in our heads than we realise and here, if you don't mind, I'll digress just a little before coming back to the main point of this section . . .

We have a conscious part to the mind and a subconscious part. The word 'subconscious' is not ideal; alternatives such as 'nonconscious' and 'unconscious' are less so. I'm not suggesting that the subconscious is in any way beneath, inferior to or less intelligent than the conscious part of the mind - it just works in a different way.

Conscious thoughts are *thoughts we know we are thinking as we think them*, for reasons we largely understand, and by an act of will - by simply making a decision - we can change our conscious thinking. The phone rings as I write this paragraph. I decide not to answer it because I'm busy . . . I knew I was thinking about the telephone as those thoughts occurred to me and I was aware of the decision I made. But then I think, 'But it might be an important call from the commissioning editor of a large publisher. Maybe I'd better answer it after all!' In other words I've changed my mind, again for reasons I'm aware of (actually it wasn't a publisher, just a cold call for website maintenance).

And that's the essence of conscious thinking. It happens in a place where we are aware of it. In order to write, streams of conscious thoughts must pass through our minds. However, that 'conscious space' is like the tip of an iceberg. There's far more going on underneath.

And that really is what I mean by the subconscious part. Subconscious thoughts are being formed but we often don't realise it at the time. However, we realise the *outcomes* of subconscious thinking. Here's an example. There's a name that you want to remember; in other words, information that you want to retrieve from your memory and bring into conscious space. The name might be on the 'tip of the tongue' as we say, but trying hard to remember that name often has the opposite result, it grows more distant; we lose it. 'It'll come to me,' we might say. Some time later, without any effort at all, the name pops into mind - *and we know it's the right name*. We know because we have the feeling that it's right, that sense of relief and satisfaction and certainty. We know too because other thoughts about the person we've remembered come to mind. Inspiration, as it were, has struck. In this case we waited for it to happen, but we can become far more systematic in putting the muse to work for us.

What we have here is a strategy which exploits the abilities of the part of the mind that operates behind the scenes, the subconscious part. Here's how to do it. We want to have ideas about our current novel, poem or play. Trying hard to force those ideas along is just plain frustrating, but waiting around for inspiration to strike is too. So . . .
- Be clear about what it is that you want to come to mind. You may already have given this some conscious thought, which is fine.
- Maintain a clear intent that these ideas, these inspirations, will soon occur to you.
- Now stop trying. Turn your thoughts away from the task and let the subconscious get on with the job.

- Allow yourself some 'downtime,' those daydreamy periods when the mind is idling and we are simply noticing ideas that rise up from the depths. This material is the result of the subconscious work that's been going on.
- As you notice this information popping into mind, notice too the sometimes subtle feelings which tell you that, yes, this fits or, no I'm not quite there yet.
- Write the ideas down at this point. This is self-respect: you are recognising your own creative abilities at this point.

You might think, it's all very well me making these claims, but does the process work? Try it and see. There are two methods you might consider.

- Seed Thoughts. Ideas, like seeds, are often full of unrealised potential. Return to the grid on page 12 and use the dice to choose two items. What link between them first comes to mind? That's a seed thought. Instead of trying consciously to turn the idea into a story, poem or whatever form you've chosen, use the strategy above. Tell yourself that in a little while you'll know far more about it. It'll come to you.

- Sleep on it. This is a variation on the above, except the subconscious work goes on while you are unconscious in sleep. Try it out; as you put your head down on the pillow each night say to yourself, 'When I wake tomorrow I'll know what my day's writing will be.' Through the night you may well dream your stories. Then, as you awake, lie quietly and notice the rich stream of ideas flowing through your conscious mind. Then reach for your notepad and pen!

Because the subconscious works holistically, rather than in linear sequences as does the conscious mind, it can be thinking about many projects at once. It's a great multi-tasking part of the mind - even in men.

7

Anchors and Filters

> The only high road to success is failure.
> *Robert Louis Stevenson*

To a large extent this book is about exploiting our wonderful resources of imagination and memory as we develop our craft. In one sense it's impossible *not* to have ideas - the mind is always busy and one thing it does naturally is to 'spin yarns,' to put ideas together into long strings. The problem sometimes is that our imaginations can run away with us, so that we have too many ideas, some of them irrelevant, some of them taking us in unintended directions.

Remember that the imagination is like a horse. It's big and powerful, but I am the rider and I have the reins. So I can run away with my imagination, but I won't let it gallop around wherever it has the whim to go. As the Chinese saying goes, 'Catch the vigorous horse of your mind.' Rein it in. Let it take you where *you* want to go.

What we need, then, are ways of reining-in the horse. Here are two ideas that I have found useful . . .

Do you sometimes find yourself 'in the mood' to write and at other times not? Wouldn't it be great to decide to get into the mood just whenever you want? Well, *anchoring* can help. An anchor is a deliberate link you make which allows you to 'switch on' creative writing at will. Many writers use this technique . . .

Ernest Hemingway supposedly sharpened a dozen pencils before writing. Sharpening those pencils got him into the mood to write.

Marcel Proust kept overripe apples in his desk drawer: the smell of the apples switched on the creative engines. My friend the late Bob Shaw, who enjoyed a glass of whisky, would place a tumblerful on the bookshelf opposite his desk. The sight of that reward was the doorway into the world of his wonderful stories.

Sometimes just sitting down in a particular place at a particular time can be enough to create an anchor that switches on the creative mindset. By why leave it to chance? Maybe you'll decide to play a certain piece of music as a prelude to your writing, or use an oil burner with different oils for 'having ideas,' 'composing ideas' and 'editing work.' Olfactory (smell) anchors can be especially powerful, since smell is processed in the same part of the brain as long-term memory. Certain aromas can evoke vivid recall and emotions (which is why perfume works).

The lovely thing about anchoring is that it's under your control, and it's cumulative. The more you use an anchor, the more powerful it becomes. When I work with children in schools, I recommend the use of a *story stone*. This is just a small pebble that you hold in your hand, telling yourself that as you hold that stone you will 'step into the world of the story and have all the good ideas you need.' It works a treat.

Another useful device for writers is *filtering*. Simply put, a filter is a particular way of seeing. Have you ever had that experience where, when you're busy working on a story, the things you see and hear around you *uncannily seem to fit your project*? That's filtering. It often happens that bits of information or quotes from books I'm currently reading are exactly what I need at that point. Similarly, if I'm developing a character the chances are that I'll meet someone who fits the bill perfectly.

One way of intensifying this experience is to pretend that you are actually in the story. I don't mean necessarily as a character, but that as you go about your day-to-day business imagine that as an interested visitor you are walking around in the world where your story happens. You may well be amazed at the fascinating spin this puts on the things you see, the people you meet, and the useful ideas you gather up. This is not some kind of supernatural phenomenon (I think), but comes down instead to the amazing abilities of your brain.

You can of course imagine that you are one of the characters in your book, and this will have the same filtering effect. Or you might adopt a pseudonym and look at the world through the eyes of your alter ego. But more on this later in the book.

Six Big Important Questions

> When the mind is at sea, a new word offers a raft.
> *Goethe*

Remember that intriguing sentence - *They shook hands, but only Baxter was smiling*? It's the kind of sentence that cries out to be questioned. This is because human beings are naturally nosy. We have a need to find out more in order to make sense of the world. It's worth bearing this in mind as we write. In creating stories we are building a world for the reader to enter, experience and enjoy. One tip for good writing, I think, is to say *just enough* to hook the reader's interest and let him do the rest of the work. The reader's own imagination will join the dots and then finish painting the picture. So always leave at least one question unanswered or something unexplained, ambiguous or uncertain until the end. The reader's natural nosiness will draw him deeper into the story to find out more.

But this is a side issue, so back to questioning. The questions prompted by 'They shook hands, but only Baxter was smiling' fall into six broad categories; Where, when, who, what, why and how. I call these the Six Big Important Questions (and I always feel compelled to capitalise those words). As authors, as creators of worlds, we need to have answers - more answers, actually, than we would ever include in the story itself.

Armed with our Six Big Important Questions, we can play the following games.

* Go back to the storylining idea on page 22. Jump in at any point

and use the coin flipping technique, focusing on each of the questions in turn. Notice how further questions spring to mind in light of the yes-no answers you get to earlier questions.

* Look again at the picture on page 18, or the new one on page 32. List as many 'where' questions as you can, then 'when' questions. . . Go through the list of six and you'll have ended up with lots of questions. You can simply decide on the answers to these, or flip the coin to think creatively on the hoof.

* When you've written your tale, use the Six Big Important Questions to do a star check. Draw a six-pointed star at random at one or two places in the story. Now look at the text in a detached way (not as your brainchild) and on the page where you've put a star ask 'Where is this event happening?' Of course you know the answer to that because you're the writer. But have you said enough in the story for the reader to have a clear impression of the setting? Now ask 'When is this event occurring?' Again, have you said enough for the reader to know when in the day or year, when in historical time, etc, the action is unfolding?

A star check is a useful review tool which links back to the idea of saying just enough to keep the reader engaged. If there's not enough detail the pictures in our head seem fuzzy and that can be a frustration: too much detail and the reader's imagination can't actively interpret and complete the world you're suggesting. It's all done for him. In that case he might as well be watching television.

If you decide to use the star check technique, also let someone else try it on your work. A fresh pair of eyes will look in a different way and may well pick out things you've missed.

Fig.4: The Mirror

32

9

Picture It

> The mind is not a vessel to be filled,
> but a fire to be kindled.
> *Plutarch*

They do say (whoever *they* are) that a picture is worth a thousand words, but it works the other way round as well. A few carefully constructed sentences can evoke the most startlingly vivid pictures in our minds *and* cause associated emotions to rise within us. The experience of reading a well-written story can be just as powerful as gazing at a brilliantly painted picture. And, for me anyway, the reading experience is dynamic: I like to move through the story guided by the sure, friendly hand of the author.

Imagery is important, as we'll see in *Visualisation*. For now let me make the point that a picture can act as a wonderful stimulus to creative writing.

★ Soft Focus/Fine Focus Noticing. Take a look at **Fig.4**, *The Mirror*, drawn by the artist Chris Pepper. Notice that you can look at it in two broadly different ways . . .

First of all, just gaze at the picture in a general way to gather the 'gist' of it. Even as we gain an overall impression our minds will be spinning yarns - You might catch yourself making up a story based on the picture, or wondering along the lines of the Six Big Important Questions. This sort of broad soft focus noticing gives us an overview.

Also be aware of any *feelings* the picture evokes in you (if it doesn't evoke any, pretend it does and notice them now).

Mentally sharpen the focus and zoom in on smaller details. Deliberately look at parts of the picture. What do you see? I have looked at this picture many times, but only today as I prepared this section did I notice the odd landscape reflected in the mirror, and deduce that the lamp above the table must be an oil- or tallow-burning lamp.

These ways of seeing offer an explanation as to why creative people sometimes wander around in a kind of daze just soaking up the atmosphere of a place, and it also perhaps accounts for the 'selective noticing' (filtering) I mentioned earlier. Either way, as we enter the imagined world of our story it changes the way the real world seems to us.

Now do this trick - Pretend the picture is in colour. Turn up the colours in your head and notice some particular ones vividly. Some people can do this effortlessly, others have to make an effort of will. But we can all do it in the end. . . And I'm not talking about logical thoughts such as 'The lamp would be a smoky yellow.' Don't just rationalise about the colour, see it.

Another piece of advice is this: if an irrational colour pops into mind - say the face of one of the figures is blue - don't simply deny it or change it. Suggest to yourself that -

Everything I think can have a useful purpose. Everything I choose to put into my story will be included for a good reason that makes the story better.

These are important principles for getting the most out of your imagination.

When you have a much clearer impression of colour, turn up the sounds in the picture and listen. Notice the overall sound in this place, then fine focus on the particulars. Imagine for instance that the man holding the mirror is speaking. Go into some detail. Be aware of the volume of his voice, its pitch, its speed, its accent. Hear it in that degree of detail, and then you'll know this character better.

Now make a leap of the imagination. Be prepared to step into the picture. Imagine you are entering that world to notice new things. What's your general impression? Now inhale. What do you smell? Touch the walls. What do they feel like. Pick up a morsel of food from the table (go on, force yourself!). Put it in your mouth - the morsel, not the table. What does it taste like? Talk with one of the shadowy figures in the background. What do you learn?

Now think to yourself, if this picture formed part of the storyline on page 22, where would it occur? What's happened to bring us up to this point? Now what happens next?

All day long and every day visual impressions stream across the mind. These are things happening outside and inside. Ultimately we don't need a picture stimulus to get us going on a story. All we need to do is visualise.

10

Visualising

> Exhilaration is that feeling you get just after a great idea hits you, and just before you realise what's wrong with it.
> *Unknown*

One of the wisest bits of advice I was ever given (I regret, I've forgotten by whom) about developing as a writer was summed up in three words - visualise, visualise, visualise! It's important right at the outset as we step into the world of the story. We need to go there and be nosy and have a multi-sensory experience. When we return to tell people about it, that's our story. We have to visit first before we can guide our readers along the same path.

Visualisation is also important on another level; on the level of composing our story word by word. Look at this:

'Running into the room, he threw open the window as he switched on the light.'

It sounds terribly dramatic, but once you picture what this character is actually doing you realise the absurdity of it. Or this:

'As a woman, James thought that she was incredibly beautiful.'

This example is as much a failure of sentence structure as a lapse of the author's ability to visualise. Generally speaking, when we visualise more clearly we can write more accurately. Here are a few more examples to tickle your funny bone . . .

- Williams saw the chaos in the street below and rubbed his nose, wondering what it would sound like.

- Like Susanna, John had dark brown hair, with enormous eyebrows, a fine moustache and handsome beard.
- Her eyes twinkled, fluttered, met his, dropped to the floor then went back to the jewels. He picked them up, held them for a moment then returned them to her with a smile.

11

50 Ideas to Boost Your Writing

Bottom-Up Top-Down Storymaking

> One of the symptoms of an approaching nervous breakdown is the belief that one's work is terribly important.
> *Bertrand Russell*

Stories, like people, are composed of many layers. Part of the fun of exploring the world we wish to write about is in considering how details of plot, character and setting rest on a platform of broader ideas. It's also the case that when we have this overview in mind we can use it as a tool for creating and constructing further pieces of work.

Imagine a pyramid divided into a number of layers, as in **Fig.5**. At the bottom, supporting everything else, are the *themes* our writing explores. Themes are often vague and wide-ranging. I think of them as being like the currents in a river, like energies that twist and swirl through human experience. Individual stories, poems and plays are like leaves scattered on the surface of the water, carried along relentlessly, each leaf affected in its own particular way by the interplay of the currents below the surface.

Themes that engage us as authors are often relevant in our own lives, although we may not realise this, sometimes even after years of writing. In my own case I had written and had published half a dozen novels before I suddenly understood that I was coming back to the same ground and working with the same themes. I saw now that among these was

- Stepping over a threshold into forbidden areas and experiencing the consequences.

Fig.5. Bottom-Up Top-Down Pyramid

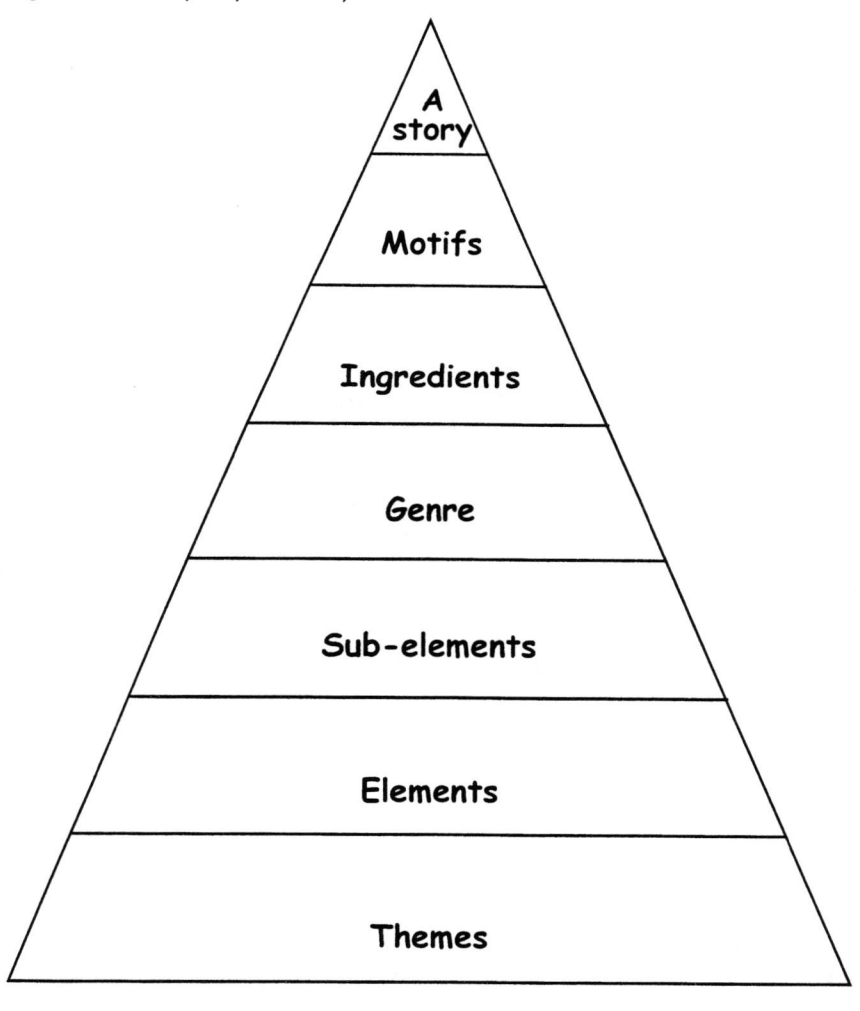

- A story
- Motifs
- Ingredients
- Genre
- Sub-elements
- Elements
- Themes

The level of all stories

- Checks and balances. 'You get nothing for nothing.' There is always a price to be paid somehow, somewhere, by someone. (This has close links with another theme that intrigues me, that of the interrelatedness of things).
- Change and transformation.
- Huge consequences arising from small and sometimes inconsequential starting points.
- Innocence and experience, usually in a spiritual and moral sense and often featuring that point in our lives when, as children, we can still see the world with an innocent eye, but we are aware too of its 'taintedness' and know the dark face of existence.

I'm sure you can appreciate that these are huge domains where ideas can germinate and flourish. Exploring just a few broad themes can occupy an author for years, and my contention is that as we learn more about such themes and why they are so personally intriguing, we come to learn more about ourselves.

Because themes are so vague and wide ranging, they can usually be broken down into 'sub themes,' smaller eddies and whirls within the larger tumbling currents of the stream. You may find that your ideas become clearer more quickly if you focus in on one or two sub themes and/or immediately begin to think of a larger theme within a particular context (linking it directly with your own life, for example).

Resting on this bed of themes are the basic structural elements that Vladimir Propp picked out so perceptively. I know I'm mixing my metaphors terribly here, but if themes are the concrete foundations of a story, structural narrative elements are the supporting girders sunk into that concrete base.

Propp went on to find that these elements could be broken down into smaller units, so-called 'sub elements.' Some of the more common are reproduced in **Fig.6**, on the next page. Again, notice

Moving away from familiar territory	The villain attempts deceipt	The hero is tested	The villain escapes	The hero goes unrecognised	The hero is recognised
An instruction is given or implied	The hero or other is deceived	A helper appears	The villain is defeated	A false hero appears	The false hero is exposed
A rule is broken	The villain causes harm	The hero acquires power	The situation is resolved	The false hero makes deceitful claims	The hero is given a new appearance
A "villain" appears	Misfortune or lack appears	The hero goes to a new place/ to search/for an object	The hero returns	A difficult task is proposed	The villain escapes
There are consequences for breaking a rule	The hero is approached with a request or command	Hero and villain meet in direct conflict	The hero is pursued	The task is undertaken	The villain is punished
The villain gains information about the hero or victim	The hero decides on action	The hero is "marked"	The hero is rescued from pursuit	The task succeeds/fails	The hero is rewarded

Fig.6: Sub-Elements Grid

that they are relatively vague, each having the potential to be used in any number of more specific ways. So, for instance, if you enjoy writing contemporary medical romances cast your eye over the sub elements grid and notice how particular situations, characters, snippets of dialogue, etc, suggest themselves. Another way of using the grid to kick-start your thinking is to choose two items randomly using dice and to place them some distance apart along a storyline (see page 22). What happens in the tale to link the first sub element with the second one?

Beyond themes and elements we come to the level of *genre*. I think of a genre as a domain within which you will conventionally find certain characters, settings and sequences of events. Personally I enjoy writing Fantasy, Science Fiction and Horror. I call them 'the three sisters' because they are closely related and share their treasures in interesting ways. A few years ago I wrote a fantasy trilogy for teenagers. It was called *The Wintering* and was set some tens of thousands of years in the future, when the Earth was passing through the next ice age. It read like high fantasy: the world was filled with gods and goddesses and supernatural events, although the reader understood that these things were the workings of advanced technology; machines that were self-maintaining. So it was also a tale of Science Fiction.

As someone once said, 'When you have learned the rules well you can bend them.' So it is at the level of genre. If you choose to write genre fiction, make sure you know it well. If you want to write Westerns, read westerns avidly, watch cowboy films, research the subject: in other words become familiar with the arena in which you are working. When you know how westerns work conventionally, you can write your own more convincingly - and then enjoy bending the rules by writing unconventional tales of the Wild West.

Another layer I consider as I build a story is that of *ingredients*. For me ingredients are not structural features in themselves;

rather they add 'flavour' to the tale, which is why I prefer the culinary metaphor. Important story ingredients include humour, tension, mystery and violence. Of course they grow out of the story itself, rather than being sprinkled on like spices, but as with chilli powder or celery salt I can add a pinch here and a pinch there to bring out the particular effect I am seeking.

Now we come to the level of *motifs*. A motif is a constituent feature that helps to define and describe the genre. Motifs, therefore, can be details of character (including stereotypes), snippets of dialogue, objects, sequences of events, details of setting and so on. A way to clarify the idea is to ask, for example, 'What makes a ghost story a *ghost* story?' ('The ghost story,' of course, being a subdivision of the Horror genre). The things that come to mind will be the motifs that allow you to identify the nature of the tale. In this case a twig tapping against a window would be a motif; or a lone figure walking along a darkened hallway, candle in hand; or a half-glimpsed movement; or the sound of running footsteps when no-one is there.

Motifs are the small-scale building blocks of the story. Most often they are used conventionally, but when you know the rules you can bend them and use motifs in a more original way.

So far I have been talking about the way narrative is built and not so much about style and the author's own unique voice in expressing the tale. This I think is something far subtler and cannot I think be taught as a series of lessons or simply by following a set of rules. I'm reminded of a story that I once heard where the great violinist Yehudi Menuhin was travelling across town in a cab to perform at Carnegie Hall. The taxi got snarled up in traffic, so Yehudi Menuhin decided to walk the last few blocks. As he hurried along, an earnest young man approached him and, obviously not recognising the great musician, said, 'Excuse me sir, but how do I get to Carnegie Hall?' Without hesitation Yehudi Menuhin said, 'Practice, my boy!'

In other words, when you've written your first million words the second million will be more powerful and will be more authentically your own.

In looking at the structural features of stories I've started at the bottom of the pyramid and worked upwards. By identifying your themes and genre first, you've already gone a long way towards organising the ideas that have occurred to you and provided yourself with a 'filter' for further thoughts. You can also approach story making from the top down: if an idea for a story pops into mind work down through the layers of the pyramid, as it were 'unpacking' the potential contained in the idea as you set it against the greater context of genre, elements and themes.

12

50 Ideas to Boost Your Writing

Creating Contexts

> Someone who carries his own lantern has no need to fear the dark.
> *Traditional saying*

Jones lay slumped on the sofa.

Curious about this? As a writer you should be. Maybe Jones is a friend of Baxter (page 18). Perhaps they were the ones who shook hands on the deal, though only Baxter was smiling. Possibly you are already 'spinning a yarn' as your creative brain, fertile with ideas, works to wrap a story around that one simple sentence.

The fact is that we *have to know*. It's in our nature. This is why we pretend to be staring out through the window of the bus or train, while actually we are listening to the conversation of two people nearby – Well, I should speak for myself really and not presume that you are as impolite as I am! Our need to know is also what propels us through a well-written story. Our readers want to find out what happens next: they do a lot of the work for us. As authors we simply need to tempt them in the right direction - which is to say, on to the next page!

However, I digress. In making a story we must create the context first, naturally enough. Earlier I showed you a few ways of doing this. Here are some more ideas:

Play the *Because Game*. This works well in a group situation, or at least with a partner so that ideas can bounce between you. Put yourself in that relaxed, easygoing state where you are not trying to figure out the right answer, but can simply notice an idea as it springs to mind. (Personally I find a large glass of red wine helps me to attain this). Now take your starter sentence. 'Jones lay slumped on the sofa . . .

Because?

Perhaps you thought 'he was tired.' That's fine. We're on our way. He was tired because? 'He'd been working late at the office.' Because? 'He needed to earn more money.' Because? 'He had to pay back Baxter.' Because? 'Baxter was blackmailing him.' Because . . .

Do you see how it works? We are exploiting our natural ability to create a context in order to find out more. And as this happens we are linking ideas together *with reasons that make sense*. This means that the whole narrative structure will hang together logically when we've finished, and as I'm sure you know, one of the things that makes a story more believable is the internal logical consistency of the world it portrays.

Within a few minutes of starting the Because Game you will have accumulated a great deal of information about Jones. But it won't just be about him. In the example above we were already starting to learn about Baxter and the sinister relationship existing between them. Half a glass of red wine and five minutes later we might have the key to the whole story, on which we can continue to build.

The chain of reasoning we were building was, however, only one chain. It's easy to go back to the starting sentence and begin again, this time suggesting that Jones and Baxter are friends. Or we might work at the level of genre and suggest that this time the Because Game using Jones lying slumped on the sofa will turn into a delightful Fantasy story for ten-year-olds. Our marvellous brains, given those instructions, will come up with the goods very easily.

A variation on the Because Game is the *Before Game*. Playing the Before Game allows us to realise at once that Jones lying slumped on the sofa is not the start of the story, but rather one frame of a movie - and we are already some way through the film. Playing the Before Game creates chronological links backwards through time; the links don't have to be strictly logical at this stage. So - Before Jones lay slumped on the sofa he . . .? 'He was making his supper.' Before he made his supper he . . .? 'He was talking with Baxter on the telephone.' Before he spoke with Baxter Jones was . . .? 'Thinking about embezzling the firm he works for.' Before these thoughts came to him he was . . .?

And so on. Because we've already played the Because Game we know why Jones was doing these things. If we'd played the Before Game first we could always create logical links between the statements by also asking 'because'?

A variation of the game is to specify particular leaps backward in time: Two weeks before Jones ever met Baxter he was? 'Enjoying a holiday with his wife.' But six months before that enjoyable holiday Jones was . . ?

Well, you can decide for yourself.

Finally let's take a look at the *While Game*. For simplicity, everything that happens in the game occurs simultaneously. There do not have to be any logical relationships between any of the things that happen (we can find those out later). But after each 'while' we step the action out distance-wise. So . . . While Jones lay slumped on the sofa, in the flat next door? 'A young couple was quarrelling.' While those young people were quarrelling, a mile away in the middle of town? 'The owner of a betting shop received a threatening phonecall.' And while that person was being telephoned, twenty miles away on the coast? 'A small powerboat was coming secretly into the bay.'

The value of this game is that it starts off with our attention focused on a small detail, that of Jones on the sofa. But then mentally we 'rise above' Jones's world and develop an increasingly wide-ranging overview. After three steps we are twenty miles away (although we can control the distance of the jump precisely each time, even to the point of stepping out yard by yard), and although the events are not linked initially, we tend naturally to put them together to create a context that makes logical sense. In my mind I was already building a scenario to do with smuggling and revenge, although this first idea is but one of many.

These simple activities encourage flexibility. We need to have the mental equipment ready if we want to write from a third person overview, or leap nimbly into the past with a flashback, or use the narrative technique of 'back story.' So even as we gather ideas for the stories themselves, we can be practising the mental skills necessary to write them most effectively.

13

50 Ideas to Boost Your Writing

Creating Convincing Characters

> The man is badly cheated who has never felt that he could not wait to get back to his work and, so feeling, hurled himself into it with fierce joy.
> *Thoreau*

For me the defining feature of a strong character is that, when you reach the end of the story, you feel as though you are leaving someone you know. In the case of sympathetic characters (the 'good guys') it's like saying goodbye to an old friend. This experience should be the same for the reader as for the author, of course.

Characters grow out of our experience of the world. We might transpose someone we know directly into a story. Or we might take a trait here, a quality there, a bundle of features from different people and weave them together to create a compound character. Or we could hijack an entire personality and distil it into someone else's body.

I've often heard it said that whatever we write about, we write about ourselves. Perhaps there is something in the idea that the characters in our stories - especially significant characters - represent facets of our own personality. If this is true in any sense, then when we go looking for inspiration for convincing characters, we also need to explore within.

Whole books have been written about character creation, so in the few pages I have allowed myself here I'd like to achieve the more modest aim of outlining a few techniques that have worked for me.

Checklist. These tips have been useful to me . . .

* Flip through a telephone directory and choose a surname and first name at random, then imagine what that person would look like.

* Notice people. Scribble down little details like the colour of someone's eyes, the shape of their mouth when they smile, the smell of the perfume or cologne they're wearing.

* Time hop. Imagine what an older person would have looked like when (s)he was younger, and vice versa.

* Listen to snippets of conversation and imagine how that conversation might continue. Notice how people speak - is the voice high or low pitched, are the words spoken quickly or slowly, are there lots of 'ahs' and 'ums' in between, the so-called 'conversational fillers'?

* Take one detail from ten different people and put them all together in a description of an imaginary character (maybe this character will work really well, but if not decide what you need to change).

* When you go shopping for clothes, look at some items that you would never wear in a million years - and imagine the person who would wear them. If you have the patience, hang around to see who actually comes along and seems attracted to those items.

* Read the work of other authors and notice how they create believable characters. Write your observations down for future reference.

* Play a piece of instrumental music that you don't know. Ask yourself 'If this music were a person, what would that person be like?'

* Imagine a 'what if' situation involving yourself such as, 'What if I found a wallet with a hundred pounds just lying there in the street?' (You can be completely honest in your thoughts because nobody will ever know!). Now imagine other responses to that situation. Let's suppose you would take the wallet to a police station. Another reaction would be to keep the money and throw the wallet away. Imagine what other characteristics such a person would possess, both physically and personality-wise.

* Look at pictures of people you don't know (that is, not famous celebrities) in newspapers and magazines and ask yourself what their typical day might be.

* If you browse around markets, bric-a-brac stores, etc, notice interesting items and wonder who might first have owned them. What kind of houses did they live in? What kind of lives did they lead?

* Notice a person you know and, in your imagination, make six changes to that person's appearance, personality or lifestyle. Write down a description of this new character.

* Remember that creating characters is not the same as characterisation. For me characterisation means imbuing a character with life within the world of the story that he or she inhabits. It's about making that character unique. The Victorian poet Gerard Manley Hopkins recognised and celebrated this idea in his concepts of 'inscape' and 'instress.' I read inscape as the 'inner landscape' of a character (though Hopkins used it to refer to every created thing). Instress for me means 'inner stress,' the dynamic tensions within characters that fits them to Somerset Maugham's definition of a human being as 'a bundle of contradictions . . .'

Practically speaking characterisation allows a character to live in the world (s)he inhabits. In a short story just a very few details might be necessary in order for that to happen. Through the course of a novel, naturally, authors have more time and space in which to work on characterisation.

Note that Hopkins' ideas can also be applied to the settings in a story. See page 71.

Vivid Particularities. This is possibly the most jargonistic phrase I'll use in the whole book! A vivid particularity is a small detail that creates a startlingly vivid picture in the imagination and makes a strong emotional impact. I'll be returning to this idea in other contexts later, but for now let's apply it to characters.

Have you had the experience of meeting someone who makes a powerful impression on you immediately? Sometimes it's the person's whole manner that comes across, but occasionally it boils down to some small quality of appearance, voice, gesture . . . Just a tiny detail which makes that person memorable. That's a vivid particularity. It may be a piece of jewellery that sets off the whole ensemble, or the kindness or vivacity of a smile; maybe the person reminds you of other times and places. Sometimes it's hard to pin down what makes someone so compelling or attractive, but as authors it's worth us taking time to notice and root out these subtle clues to that individual's charisma.

It works in the negative too. Within a few moments of meeting a stranger we might dislike him or her intensely, and again it might boil down to a small mannerism or other trait that, for whatever reason, really irritates. But in the world of writing 'everything is material,' so however much we are annoyed or repulsed by another, it pays to take the time to learn more; sometimes to sit in quiet reflection and let memories rise, and to use our intuition to learn more about our deeper selves.

Briefly put, then, whatever striking details make an impact on you, note them down and use them to make your characters live.

Character Types. There are stereotypes and there are what I call 'character types.' A stereotype is a 'character cliché,' someone used off the peg without much thought about how to make them individuals. Even major characters, if they are stereotypes, tend to be shallow and tokenistic. Except in a few instances stereotypes are to be avoided. Because they are not the products of reflection, they reflect badly on the author.

The instances I'm thinking about are: a) if a stereotype is used ironically, b) if the stereotype is used, again deliberately, with the addition of vivid particularities, which add to his or her individuality, c) in some genre fiction (usually Science Fiction or Fantasy) where there exists the notion of 'idea as hero.' In this case the *raison d'être* of the story is the expression or explanation of a technological or supernatural idea, to which the characters and even settings and plot devices can be subservient. So, to take a dreadfully unoriginal example, if I wrote a story where a scientist goes back in his once-only time machine to bring back the only (now dead) surgeon who can save his terminally-ill wife - but the time machine lands on the surgeon and kills him - the central idea of the story is what the story is all about. There is nothing else. The characters of the scientist and surgeon are tokens, and so I think can legitimately be stereotypes in these circumstances.

Character types, on the other hand, are individuals that grow over time, perhaps during the course of a single story or, indeed, over many. Central figures in detective fiction provide some immediate examples. But character types can also appear as different people in different tales, all of whom have their roots in one individual who has become significant to the author.

In my own writing I use two character types regularly. One of them is a boy of around eleven years old. I often call him Tony. He is introverted, shy, very bright, intuitive, and often comes up with a brilliant plan to save the day. My other character type is usually called Eleanor (never 'Ellie,' she hates that). She's between thirteen and sixteen, tall, thin, has fair hair and most boys find her attractive although Eleanor never believes them. She's full of self-doubt. She also usually has some physical deformity, which feeds her doubt and lack of confidence. In one story she had a withered hand, in another she was losing her sight. Eleanor only discovers her strength when she is tested to her limits. This usually occurs at the story's denouement.

For me the lovely thing about character types is that you get to visit them many times and, like true brainchildren, you have the pleasure of watching them grow.

Names. I wonder if a rose by any other name would smell as sweet? Objectively it might, but I suspect that if it were called a carrion-flower my subjective impression would be adversely affected.

Characters' names can be a real sticking point. There are a number of ways of tackling this issue.

* Never try hard to make up a character's name, as it often sounds forced and artificial. On my reference shelf I have dictionaries of first names and the local telephone directory. I might choose a first name according to its traditional meaning or, more intuitively, simply because it seems to suit the character I have in mind. I chose 'Eleanor' for instance because it somehow seemed to fit her personality. I subsequently discovered that it derives from Helen, which means 'the bright one.' So I was doubly pleased.

* An extension of this idea is if you are basing a character very solidly on a real person. I find that I have to use that person's

actual name. A character type I've used in several books is a rather plump self-conscious girl called Katie. I found that if I wrote about her by the name I'd chosen for her in the story, the job was much harder. So I simply called her 'Katie' and then, when the story was finished, replaced it with her 'fictional' name.

* Play around with matching up first names and surnames. Do it randomly twenty times and you might come up with a name that's just right.

* If you are writing Fantasy or Science Fiction, you might try the following techniques . . .

- Take an ordinary name and play about with it. Brian can turn into Brin, Bren, Bran, etc. Put a vowel at the end. Briana, Brianu. Put a vowel in front. Ubrian. Ibrian. Do both. Ibrianu, etc.

- Chose a polysyllabic word such as 'unafraid.' Chunk it into smaller blocks of letters. Una, Nafrai, Raiduna. Look at it back to front. Iarfa, Anu, Arfanu.

- Take a line of text and match up the last syllable of one word with the first syllable of the next. Using the line before this one we get; Kea, Ali, Neo, Ofte, Xtan, Andma, and so on.

- Books of obscure myths and legends often feature many names that carry few associations and that not many people will know.

I'll have more to say about names later when we look at pseudonyms, but for now, let's dig deeper into characters.

14

Top-Down Bottom-Up Characters!

> Knowledge is vain and full of error
> when it is not born of experience.
> *Leonardo da Vinci*

Let me add quickly that the heading is not intended as a *double entendre*! I simply wanted to make the point that the pyramid organiser we used to think about narrative structure is also useful in the context of developing characters. Refer to **Fig.7**.

Recording information in this way makes the point - and keeps it in front of the eye - that people have depth. We are layered. I also happen to think that the lower layers influence the upper layers more than the other way round. So, I would suggest that our basic motivations are what drive us through life; the words motives, move and emotions derive from the same root. These also define our values which, in turn, clarify our goals and ambitions. My contention is that the way we envisage our personal future gives meaning to our background: as someone once said, it's not what's happened to us that counts, but how we *use* what's happened to us. In a very profound sense all of this amounts to a powerful energy rising from the core to give shape to the personality, which in turn affects our appearance in many ways.

The pyramid organiser is a constant reminder of the points above as our characters take shape. If you draw the pyramid on a sheet of A4 paper you'll appreciate that there's not much room to make notes. This is a benefit rather than a limitation, because it forces us to choose and prioritise the information. It's all too easy to

Fig.7: Character Pyramid

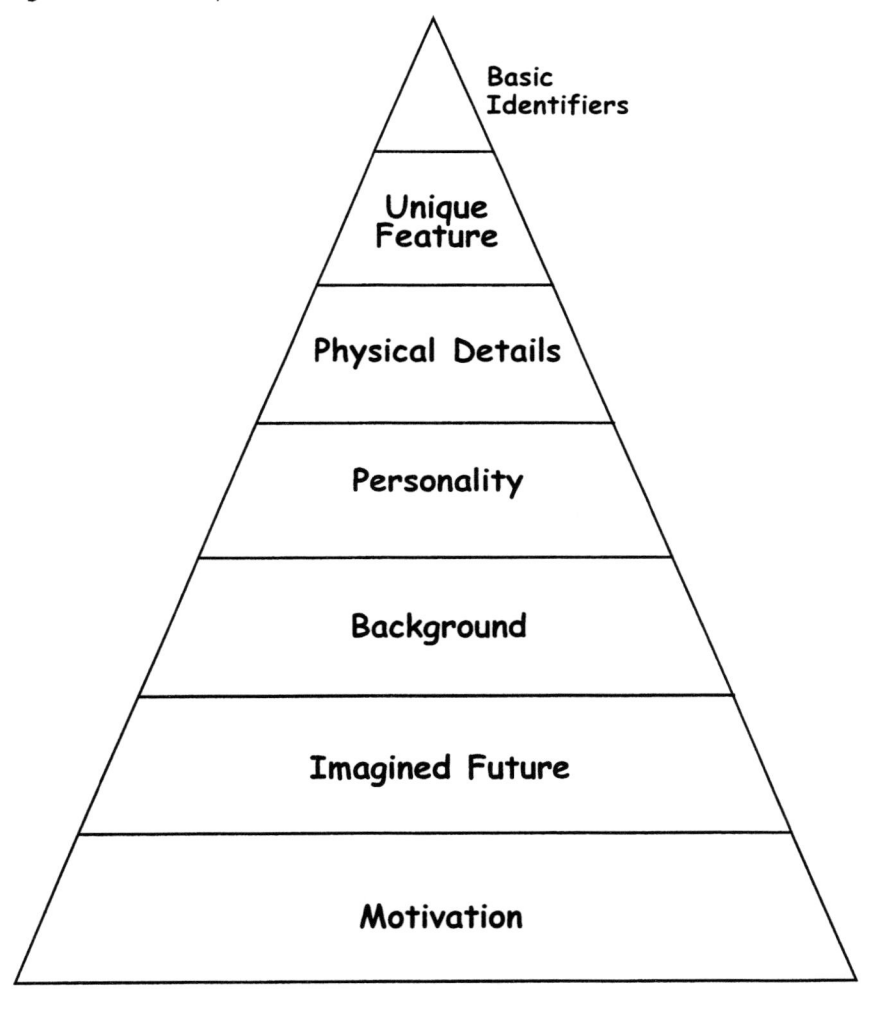

- Basic Identifiers
- Unique Feature
- Physical Details
- Personality
- Background
- Imagined Future
- Motivation

become cluttered up with details - and although you might argue that as authors we need to know everything about our characters, we don't need to make much of it explicit; the rest informs the writing without itself being stated.

The pyramid organiser is largely self-explanatory, but let me clarify a few things here.

- Basic identifiers. These are the two or three details that 'tag' the character from the outset. So if you imagine your character walking in to the room for the first time, what few things would you say about him or her?

- Unique feature. This is usually a 'vivid particularity,' something unique to that individual. The detail might be drawn from any other section of the pyramid, so it could be some future achievement, or a thought, or an aspect of the personality which may not yet even have expressed itself. I usually fill this section in last, when my knowledge of the character is more extensive.

You don't need to complete a pyramid in order to feature that character in your story. Your working method might be to let your characters 'take on a life of their own,' so that you learn about them as the story develops. In this case, you can add details to the pyramid as you go without losing the 'big picture' of what makes each character tick.

One interesting use of this technique, practised perhaps in a group situation, or if you have already created a number of pyramids, is to put two or more together and imagine them in conversation. Would they like each other or not? And why? How might they change in light of the meeting? If they met each other again in five years' time, how would each have changed?

15

50 Ideas to Boost Your Writing

Back to the Starting Grid

> But in vain we build a world
> unless the builder also grows.
> *Eando Binder*

The grid on page 12 can be of use to us again here, as we think about a character's personality. For instance, if the following image told us something about a positive personal quality our character possesses, what would we learn?

Your response might be perseverance and determination, stable, good at overcoming obstacles. Now if the same image told us something about a *negative* attribute, what might it be? In workshops people have said flawed, fractured, unapproachable. It all depends on how we look at things.

The power of the imagination allows us to think and perceive metaphorically. We can take any object and use it to represent something else. This I suppose is the basis of symbolism. For our present purposes, we can now look at the image grid and imagine it as a 'personality map,' not just for one character that you're developing, but for your entire *dramatis personae*.

One way of getting started is to roll the dice twice to choose an image at random and suggest to yourself that it will tell you 'something about' your character. That phrase is wonderfully vague and encourages your subconscious imagination to create an idea without you having to struggle logically to work out what the image should mean. At this stage of gathering ideas or envisioning characters, events, etc, it's more productive to let inspiration work behind the scenes. Later, when we have lots of material to work with, is the time to apply conscious logical thinking in deciding which ideas we'll weave into the final work.

Another way of approaching the grid is to use the PIN technique - Positive, Interesting, Negative. Use the dice to select an image. This tells you something positive about your character. Roll the dice again. Now you learn something 'interesting' (interpret that as you like!). A third dice roll selects an image that highlights a negative attribute of the character. Continue cycling through the PIN technique until you have learned as much as you need to at this stage. A slightly more challenging exercise is to choose an image and use it to tell you something positive *and* interesting *and* negative about the character.

What you learn by using the grid will help you to fill in the sections of the character pyramid. I'm sure you'll appreciate that you can use the techniques above to learn more about the character's background, imagined future (ambitions, dreams), motivations - in fact any aspect of that person's life.

If the grid and pyramid ideas appeal to you and you are prepared to return to them a number of times, you can use your knowledge of one character to fire up your imagination to create others. Have a few pyramid blanks ready as you consult the grid - which you might do by using the dice or simply by choosing images for yourself. Based on what you know of your initial character . . .

- What would that person's best friend be like in terms of looks, personality, etc?

- What would your first character's worst enemy be like?
- What would your character's male/female equivalent be like?
- If your character became a mother/father, what blend of characteristics would the first born child possess?
- Choose a story that you've enjoyed in the past (film, novel, or whatever). Imagine your chosen character as the hero or villain in that story. A) How would the presence of your character change the story? B) How would your character have changed by the end of the story?

16

50 Ideas to Boost Your Writing

Bundles of Contradictions

> Curiosity has its own reason for existing.
> *Albert Einstein*

It was Somerset Maugham who, when asked to define a human being said 'Any person is a bundle of contradictions.' That of course is what makes people interesting (and positive and negative), both in fiction and in life. If the hero of a story were thoroughly, completely good and noble he'd be rather dull I think. Similarly a villain with absolutely no redeeming feature would not be so intriguing or so powerful a character as one where there existed some spark of remorse or kindness.

I feel that as authors we need to bear in mind the complexity of all of the characters we create - certainly the main characters, but even ones who make only fleeting appearances should be informed by the author's deeper knowledge of them. Another feature of stereotypes is that they lack this kind of depth. They are tokens, used unthinkingly, by lazy writers.

The pyramid technique by its very nature encourages us to think about the layeredness of the characters that populate our stories. Another way of creating more convincing characters is to use a template like the one in **Fig.8**. This is a fairly simple example. You can add to the list endlessly. Notice that I've chosen some deliberately ambiguous terms. 'Smart' for instance could mean smart in appearance or clever - in which case, how is 'smartness' different from intelligence or cunning? The terms we choose generate a positive pressure for us to think further about their

Fig.8: A Bundle of Contradictions

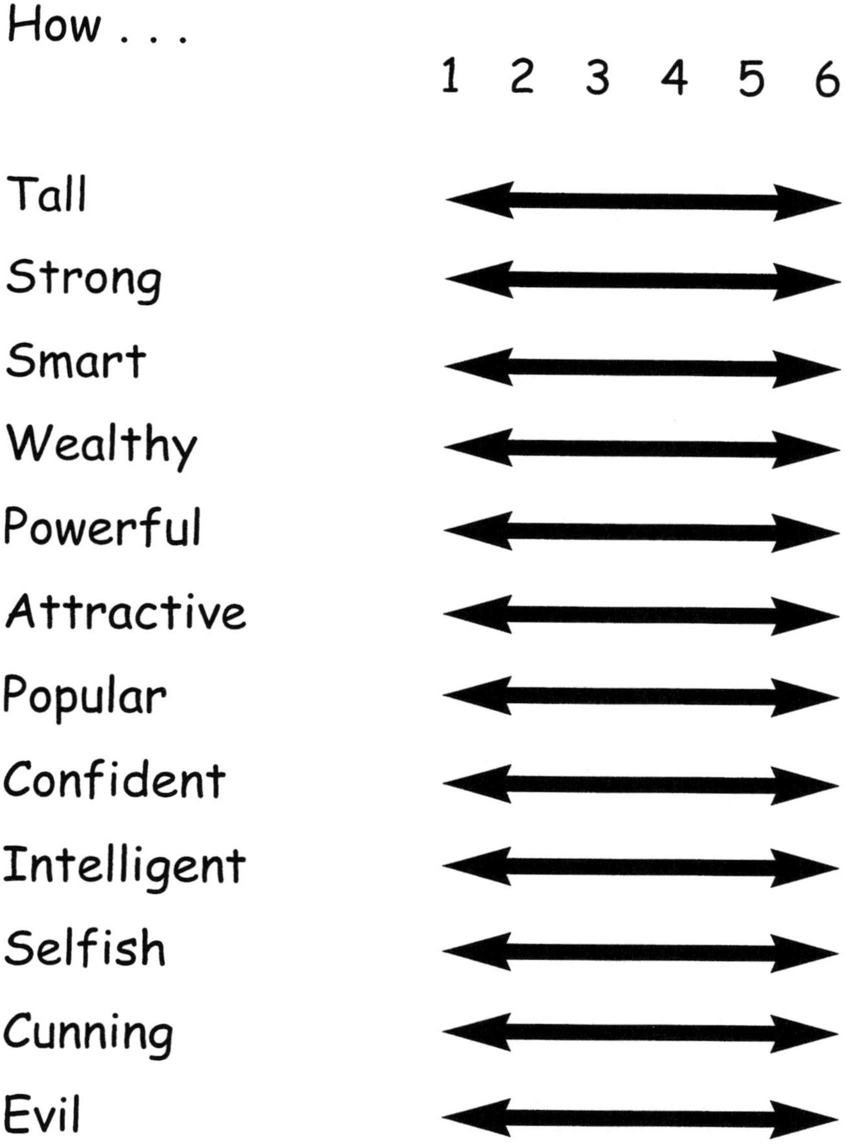

How . . .

	1	2	3	4	5	6
Tall	←―――――――――→
Strong	←―――――――――→
Smart	←―――――――――→
Wealthy	←―――――――――→
Powerful	←―――――――――→
Attractive	←―――――――――→
Popular	←―――――――――→
Confident	←―――――――――→
Intelligent	←―――――――――→
Selfish	←―――――――――→
Cunning	←―――――――――→
Evil	←―――――――――→

meanings. This can only be a good thing, since language is the raw material of our craft.

Using the numbers 1-6 allows you to make a mark along the line as you decide on a particular quality or attribute for your character. You'll appreciate that the numbers are not precise and objective units of measurement but comparative indicators of your subjective judgement. So if you ask 'How tall will my character be?' and you opt for 4, this does not mean that person is four feet tall, but rather that she's a little taller than average. This distinction becomes obvious when we ask a question such as 'How wealthy will my character be?' Compared to whom? Compared to most authors, probably five or six. Compared to the most successful authors, undoubtedly 'one'!

As with the pyramid organiser, this technique allows you to keep track of the decisions you make about your characters as they take shape. Make a mark on each line and, when you've gone down the list, you have a quick visual reference of your character's profile. Here are a few ideas to extend your use of the template.

* Use the dice to choose characteristics randomly. You are then much more likely to end up with a bundle of contradictions. It becomes an enjoyable and useful creative challenge to explain how a character might, for instance, be popular (6) and confident (1), or powerful (5) and selfish (6). Simply picking two characteristics to rationalise can immediately suggest scenarios or even whole storylines.

* Alternatively roll the dice and make your own decision. So, the dice indicates that your character is wealthy (4). Now you decide on how powerful he or she would be.

* Use the dice to create a random profile. Now deliberately alter one of the values and ask yourself, 'Which other characteristics

would change? And by how much? And why?' By this time you are really getting to know your character well!

* Create a profile by making decisions. This represents your character now. Create a second profile using the dice. This represents your character at some time in the past or future. What has happened/will happen to account for the differences?

17

It's All in the Mind

> Thank you for your advice.
> I shall lose no time in taking it.
> *Benjamin Disraeli*

The writer Anais Nin once said that we see the world not as it is, but as *we are*. This profound idea offers insight to us as authors. And I'm using the word 'insight' deliberately, for we need to look in to find out. The whole art of visualisation means looking in to our own minds as we represent the world of the story in the imagination. Similarly, in creating convincing characters we must - as far as we can - step into their shoes and see the world from their perspective. We might all look at a chair and agree that it is a chair, but perhaps it reminds me of the chair that was the favourite of my bullying great uncle whose blustering voice and intimidations terrified me. Maybe you have fond memories of a similar chair and regard it with nostalgic fondness. We may all look upon the same object, but each of us will see it differently.

Characters grow as we use them in our stories, but before we ever sit down to begin chapter one, page one we can - and should - gather up some insights as to how the world looks from their perspective.

* Decide on a character's star sign and write her horoscope.

* Imagine in detail what her kitchen would look like.

* Create a character envelope. Put inside the envelope ten items associated with the person you have in mind. (This, by the way, makes for an interesting writers' group activity. Each member of the group creates a character envelope; then exchange

envelopes and write a description of the person the items suggest).

* Be your character for a day. Social convention might influence how far you can go with this! But at least endeavour to see the world from her point of view. What opinions does she hold about the things you encounter? What does she think of your friends? What does she think of you?

* Create a grid like the one below, **Fig.9**. List your characters as shown. Then have two characters 'jump into' a box. What would their first impressions be of each other? What might they say? If each could ask the other a significant question, what would it be?

* Now take a look at **Fig.10**. I call this activity 'The World Inside.' Imagine that these are the thoughts going on inside the mind of a twelve-year-old boy . . .

Fig.9: Cross-match Characters

	Character A	Character B	Character C	Character D
Character A				
Character B				
Character C				
Character D				

Fig.10: The World Inside

- Why is he thinking of these things? And why is he thinking of them in this way? This game encourages active 'mind reading' as you interpret what's on the character's mind.

- A variation of the game is to select one item from the circle and to describe how different characters in your story would see it (If you have artistic abilities you can draw the different interpretations). So if we choose, for example, the image of the child at the computer. The little boy represents it this way, perhaps, because 'computers make him feel small.' Another character might see the computer screen as a doorway opening on to a wonderful landscape.

- Based on what the little boy is thinking, write a description of him. Or, more adventurously, fill in a character pyramid.

- If you really want to get into this character, imagine you are the small boy and invite your friends to ask you/him some questions. Notice how the answers often pop easily into mind.

18

A Sense of Place

> She'll wish there were more,
> an' that's the great art o' . . . writin'.
> *Dickens, Pickwick Papers*

The setting of a story is often fundamental to the whole creation rather than being simply an interesting or colourful background. The great British ghost story writer M. R. James, for instance, made effective use of the bleak flat landscapes of the East Anglia coast while - I'm sure you'll agree - many of Conan Doyle's Sherlock Holmes adventures would not be the same if they hadn't been set in fog-bound London. Memorable settings, as with memorable characters, have a richness, depth and uniqueness to them which, when drawn out through good writing, gives the reader an experience of having *been there*.

In the world of writing I often come across the advice to 'write what you know.' What this means to me changes according to the context. I like to write Science Fiction, Fantasy and Horror. I've never met a vampire (as far as I know), but if that character represents the outsider, loneliness, compulsion, hunger, then exploring that character also allows me to explore those themes, to which we are all connected as human beings. Landscapes, however, are different I think. True enough, they can be used metaphorically or iconically - I can set my science fiction story of alien invasion in the Arizona desert, as so many 1950s American movies did, without ever having visited* - but if I create a character who's an amateur detective in her spare time, when not running the post office and shop in a quaint Rutland village, then I really need to know that place for my writing about it to be informed. Clearly, writing what you know is not always the same as personal experience; but in all cases it should be *informed* at some level.

(* The desert was not too far from Hollywood, and location filming out there was cheap!)

The superb Victorian poet Gerard Manley Hopkins (in common with other great spiritual writers such as the modern poet R. S. Thomas) used landscape as an expression of God's creative power. In refining his thinking Hopkins also developed the fascinating concepts of *inscape* and *instress*. Inscape is the inherent uniqueness of a place, right down to the trees and stones you find there, each tiny thing contributing to the specialness of the whole. Instress is the expression of that specialness, the 'breathing forth' * of the inscape; things 'selving,' being themselves. Much of his poetry and the entries in his journals strove to catch the inscape of a place at the moment of its impression upon the eye and the heart. This has links for me with the ancient notion of the genius loci, the spirit of a place, which is drawn out ('breathed forth') by the presence of the observer.

(* The roots of the word 'inspiration' take us back to the same thing, a breathing in of experience, a breathing forth of what that experience means to us individually).

All of the above contributes usefully, I think, to what I mean by a sense of place. What words do we choose to convey that sense, as apart from simple descriptions of buildings and trees, patterns of clouds and references to the weather? Broadly speaking I feel that if we become increasingly sensitive to it - if we see as a child does, with what the educationalist Margaret Meek calls 'firstness' - then we will be guided by our experience and the right words will suggest themselves.

In practical terms simply to linger in a place and quietly notice our own thoughts, feelings and impressions will help. To 'be here now' connects us with our environment. What do we experience in the moment as participants in the inscape of a place? What sensory details catch the imagination? We need to know, because these are the details we might well choose to put into the writing to recreate that experience for the reader.

Think back to the picture work we did earlier. My encouragement was to explore with all of the senses; to see with the mind's eye, hear with the mind's ear, touch with the mind's hands. The difference now, as we simply 'stand and stare,' is that the landscape comes to us: we have no need to probe actively with the imagination at this point, but simply to notice and, later, to tell.

Give some attention to the sense of smell. I smell often (if you take my meaning). Physiologically, the olfactory (nose) nerve runs directly to the part of the brain responsible for emotions and long term memories. I was born and raised in the Rhondda Valleys of South Wales and even now, decades after moving away, the smoky smell of a coal fire drops me straight back into my childhood. Sometimes a brief reference to smell as part of your description of a place can make a world of difference.

19

50 Ideas to Boost Your Writing

Focus of Attention

> May you live all the days of your life.
> *Jonathan Swift*

On a technical level, how might we set about composing a description of a place? Our words will direct the reader's focus of attention, so obviously we need to be aware of our own focus of attention as we reach for the words we wish to use. 'Being aware of being aware' is a defining feature of human consciousness, and certainly of competent writing as far as I'm concerned.

We'll use the picture on page 32 as our example. You've looked at it closely before, so as you take it in now (to get ready to 'breathe it forth'), what second impressions come to mind? Perhaps it's stating the obvious to suggest that what strikes you initially might not be the impressions you want the reader to experience first. Remember that composing your description doesn't simply mean writing down your thoughts in the order in which they occur to you. And it's also the case that our description of place is embedded in a larger fiction. We want it to set the scene, of course, but also to blend with and enhance what we'll say about our characters, as we move the story along.

Let's exercise the imagination. Instead of focusing on details, 'defocus' to take in the entire thing as an overview. In a sentence, how might we describe our general impression of that tavern room as we build it into the story? Here are a few ideas that came to my mind . . .

- The tavern's bare wooden walls had soaked up three hundred

years of noise, but now silence lay oppressively in the air; no man dared to speak.
- As Ibrien stared into the mirror, the room's close confines became even more oppressive. Unafru felt trapped inside the cone of light cast across the table.
- One man among the onlookers shifted his weight and a bare board creaked. Everyone in the old tavern was staring at Ibrien as he gazed into the mirror unlike all other mirrors - for it was not reflecting his face.
- The old wooden walls and the scrubbed tables and low beamed roof of the tavern had heard countless tales of magic. But now, here, on this night, the truth had been revealed.

I can slip into 'editor mode' by detaching myself from trying to describe the room and look back with a critical eye at what I have done. I notice from my attempts above that my general impression features the room's oppressiveness, its age and the 'worn-ness' of the wooden walls, floor and furniture. As the creator of the work, is that what I intend? If so, then I can settle on one of the sentences above or compose something new based on my insight. For me that's what authorship means - while part of me becomes lost in the world of the story, another part of my mind looks on with a cool and calculating eye and chooses the right words to convey what I'm experiencing. Further drafting refines those impressions.

I also notice that my overview included sound (and lack of it) and my impression of the age of the tavern, but made no mention of colour. Now I might wish to incorporate that and perhaps smell and touch, although bearing in mind that description can be ruined by too many references.

The reader's attention can also, of course, be finely focused on small details through any of the bodily senses. To practise this, go into the picture again and describe a detail of something you can see, hear, touch, smell. You do not necessarily need to write a sentence as you would use it in a story: a bare impression will do.

- I noticed food crumbs on the table, bits of bread crust.
- I heard the sputtering of the wick in the lamp.
- I rubbed the tablecloth between my thumb and index finger and found it to be made of coarse linen.
- I smelt a meaty, 'vinegary' stink from the dinner plates.

With a leap of the imagination we can also notice details from any point of view. What, for instance, can the 'skull faced' character in the background see that we cannot from our perspective? Linked to this technique are the decisions we make about whether to describe the scene in a more detached and objective way (1), or from the subjective 'inner world' viewpoint of one of the characters (2), or using third person narrative overview that incorporates what characters think (3).

1. The three men sat around the table that was still littered with the remnants of the simple meal that they had recently finished.

2. It angered me that Ibrien and the others had shown no appreciation of the food they'd eaten. Life had always been hard for me. Fresh bread and cheese was a luxury, even now. I wanted to scoop up the crumbs and other morsels they'd left lying, but that of course would incur the most terrible consequences . . .

3. Life had always been hard for the warrior, Unaf. Standing back, keeping his distance and his silence amongst the other Protectors, his eyes nevertheless were fixed hungrily upon the morsels of food that Ibrien and his guests had left lying on the tavern table . . .

The wording of example 1 also raises the question of 'author intrusion'. An objective narrative overview should be just that, a detached telling where no trace of the author's own opinions 'leak' into what is said. With that in mind, the words 'still littered' could suggest that I, as the author, have expressed the opinion that the remnants of the meal should have been cleared away by now! Sometimes it's a hard and subtle judgement to make. My own opinion (which I am pleased to intrude here) is that the occasional less obvious or clumsy intrusion is allowable if it contributes to the style and 'flavour' of the writing, whereas glaring examples or the overuse of what-the-author-thinks should be avoided. A compromise that's sometimes useful is to tell the tale from the viewpoint of a narrator-character, someone who's passing on the story. In that case you can have both the narrative overview and added dimension of the narrator's own commentary, judgements, humour and opinions.

Another technique for description of place is the 'filmic' way of doing things. If your story were a movie how might you, as director, guide the camera's eye?

- You might zoom in from a great height. Perhaps a raven drops down from the heavens towards the tiny spark of the light lost in the darkness of the countryside, perching at last at an open window to hear what's being said.
- You can start with a close-up of the strange landscape reflected in the mirror, moving out slowly to take in the trembling hand of Ibrien, then the supper table, Ibrien's companions, the watching crowd . . .
- Or start with a view of Unaf and pan around the room.
- Or 'track in' from the doorway of the tavern, moving into the room as a newcomer might do, finding yourself confronted with the central tableau of the scene.

- Or start with a brief description of the landscape in the mirror as though you were there, then move out through the mirror into the 'other world' of Ibrien.

In fact there are many possibilities. But this simply reflects the craft of writing. Sentence by sentence we are confronted by endless choices and are required to make thousands of decisions. Experienced authors do this swiftly, effectively and with relatively little conscious effort. The words simply flow out on to the screen or page, just as an accomplished musician's hands 'know what to do' so that the music plays itself. And perhaps this notion brings us full circle. When I have a sense of what I want to say, I can let the writing take over, sit back and enjoy the view.

20

Jigsaw Town

> You give birth to that on which you fix your mind.
> *Antoine de Saint-Exupery*

Sometimes only a particular place will work as the setting for your story. Perhaps the romance *must* happen against the dramatic scenery of the North Cornish coast, or the crime has to be committed on London's Oxford Street on a warm May evening. This kind of decision is almost always more than just the author's whim or the lazy option of using a stereotypical setting. Often a place is used deliberately because the author knows it well and has absorbed its atmosphere: the 'spirit of place' has soaked into the bones. Some of my favourite children's fantasy stories would lose some of their power if the setting were different. Alan Garner's classic *Elidor*, for example, effectively uses the contrast between the magical realm of Elidor and the urban sprawl of 1960s Manchester. John Gordon's evocative story *The Giant Under the Snow* makes great use of snow-bound Norwich, with a dark undertow of evil unfolding beneath the façade of pre-Christmas tinsel and busy shopping streets.

On the other hand the science fiction writer Douglas Hill loves to create his own worlds from scratch. Doug maintains that because they are entirely his he can do what he likes in them and no-one can argue - provided the worlds are logically consistent. If he wants the mountains to be pink, that's fine, as long as the pinkness exists for a reason that makes sense and contributes positively to the story.

Again it's a matter of choice. Sometimes the solution lies in the creation of what I call a 'jigsaw town,' a setting which has been built from bits and pieces of other places. Stephen King uses this technique extensively in the form of Castle Rock. In my own case, I frequently set my stories in a town called Kenniston. Parts of it closely resemble the market town in Leicestershire close to where I live. However, I've made the surrounding hills higher so that they look like the upland scenery of the Welsh valleys where I grew up. On the East side, just past the Ridge Road, there sprawls Patchley Woods, which are always dark and mysterious and exciting and where lots of magical and frightening things can happen. Several years ago I felt compelled to draw a map of Kenniston so that I could be consistent in my use of it. These days I visit often and in all kinds of weather, just to see what I'll discover.

Making up a jigsaw town is great fun and becomes an increasingly useful convenience if a 'real world' particular location is not vital to the story. I suppose such a jigsaw town is analogous to a 'character type' (see page 53): it's a place that evolves in the author's mind and, as time goes by, acquires its own spirit and uniqueness.

21

50 Ideas to Boost Your Writing

The Colour of Saying

> A crank is a person with a new idea -
> Until it catches on.
> *Mark Twain*

Imagine the smell of fireworks and, at the same time, notice any other thoughts and feelings you may experience. Now here's the challenge - If I had never smelt fireworks before in my life, how would you describe that smell to me?

Description relies upon some kind of cross-match of meaning between the writer and reader. Whatever experience an author offers us, it has to connect with us at some point, at some level. How did you tackle your challenge? Some ways of evoking a new experience are:

* By memory, perhaps describing a bonfire that you recall in the hope that the reader has at least been to something similar.

* By direct association, comparing the smell of bonfire smoke to some other kind of smoke - smoke from a coal fire maybe, or the smoke of a steam train.

* By comparison (less direct association), using similes and metaphors to represent the smoke as something more familiar to the reader. This may also involve association and memory. 'Firework smoke smells like hot chestnuts, bright sparks, childlike excitement, wide eyes - all wrapped up in a freezing November night.'

Another technique is to describe the smoke *synaesthesically*, which means in terms of other physical senses. I vividly remember a writing workshop I was running in a primary school and this very problem came up - describing the smell of fireworks. One young girl struggled to summon the words and eventually abandoned the effort, shrugged and said, ' Well it's quite a nice smell.' I said to her, 'What if you could touch the smell of the fireworks? Reach out and touch it now. What does it feel like?' Her hand lifted and she said very definitely, 'It's soft and fluffy.' 'All right,' I continued, 'pretend the smell is a musical sound. What do you hear?' 'It's quiet, a humming sound.' 'And if the smell had a colour, what would it be? What colour do you imagine right now?' She told me very confidently that she saw light purple.

So we were able to agree that the fireworks had a soft, fluffy, quietly humming light purple smell. This is a far richer and more original description than 'It's quite a nice smell.' And that's what synaesthesia is about, describing one sensory impression in terms of others. It's a kind of metaphor, but such cross-matching of senses is deeply built into the way our brains work, allowing us to make 'senses' of the world in an elegant and sophisticated way.

The phenomenon of synaesthesia has only in recent years been appreciated as a powerful, natural ability, but it has existed probably for as long as human consciousness. Certainly our language is littered with synaesthesic references. Ask ten people what colour rage is and most or all of them will know. In this case the reference most likely goes back to the literal reddening of the skin as anger rises. Less well known, but just as relevant, are the terms 'blue funk,' 'brown study' - and what about 'purple prose'?

As a technique for writing, I feel that synaesthesic descriptions are most effective when used occasionally. They should sparkle like stars across the scape of the work rather than hitting the senses every other paragraph. Now that you are aware of 'the colour of saying' (to use a term coined by Dylan Thomas), I'm sure you'll notice many kinds of cross-matches in the fiction you read. And before moving on in your own writing, answer me this . . .

- How would you describe the taste of a cherry?
- What colour is the texture of silk?
- If you could hold the ringing of church bells, what would that feel like?
- What does a sunrise taste like?
- What's the difference in shape between the cry of a seagull and the call of an owl?
- If your favourite piece of instrumental music were a person, what would that person look like?

22

Emotional Impact

> They conquer who believe they can.
> *Ralph Waldo Emerson*

One important criterion of any powerful communication is when the writer's intention to create an emotional impact is matched by the reader's response. Plainly put, if I write a ghost story and my intention is to chill you - *and I do*, then I have succeeded. That link between intention and effect guides me constantly as I endeavour to put one word sensibly in front of another.

Emotion - motive - motivate - movement; emotions underpin everything that we do as human beings, not just as writers. The way we feel about the craft is fundamental to our achievement and any commercial success that may come our way. It is beyond the scope of this book to dwell substantially on the topic, important though it is, but I would like to offer a few ideas at this point which, I hope, will help to round off the first half of *50 Ideas to Boost Your Writing* and springboard us into the second.

* Examine your own motives for writing. I trust that you write because you love it. I only met one commercially successful writer who did it for the money and, not coincidentally I think, he was one of the most miserable souls I've ever encountered.

* Be aware of emotions that you think limit your progress. Be open and honest with yourself and name those demons. One way of dealing with limiting feelings is to use the power of your own imagination. Pick a limiting feeling. Pretend you could reach out and touch it. What does it feel like? Give it a colour. Imagine you

can tap it with your pen. What sound does it make? Scratch the feeling with a penknife and sniff the aroma. Locate it somewhere inside yourself. Where is it most troublesome?

You have now defined that feeling synaesthesically. Do the next bit quickly, without bothering to analyse the process or doubt it. Swiftly change the colour, texture, weight, temperature, sound, odour and location of the feeling. Stick it somewhere silly - on your head or your knee, or on the end of your big toe. Now imagine you can grab hold of it, scrunch it up and toss it away like litter.

* By the same token, anchor positive feelings. I use a 'story stone.' This is just a small pebble. Whenever I feel a sense of achievement in my work; when I am pleased with a paragraph or sentence, when I receive a compliment - and certainly when I sign a publisher's contract! - I'll hold the story stone in my right hand and therefore link it mentally with those good feelings. If, subsequently, a setback threatens or if I have a lapse of confidence, I'll take hold of that story stone and remember the good feelings all over again. And here I'm using the word 'remember' very precisely; to 're-member,' to recreate in the members, in the flesh, the positive feelings I have associated with the stone.

* With regard to the above, and in thinking about your characters' emotions, give some thought to the sometimes subtle distinctions between feelings. How would you describe the difference between unease and apprehension? If rage is red, what colour is fury? Why? Make a graph. The horizontal line represents frequency or 'commonness,' with rarer emotions tending towards the right. Make a mark halfway up the vertical line. Anything above will be a positive emotion, anything below will be a negative emotion. The further above or below the mark you put an emotion, the more powerful it will be. Something like 'bliss' therefore would be positioned towards the top right-hand

corner of the graph, since it is powerfully positive but rarely experienced. Discriminating between emotions in this way and the huge vocabulary naming and describing them makes us more precise in our writing. We will become less inclined to use casual superlatives and, I suggest, more elegant in the way we achieve an emotional impact in our readers.

23

50 Ideas to Boost Your Writing

Stuff and Nonsense

> To become a successful writer you must take your backside and put it on a seat - every day.
> P. G. Wodehouse (attrib.)

We have already explored the notion of a sense of place. It is powerful but subtle, always there but easily missed unless we work to refine our perceptions and sensibilities to notice it. In this segment I'd like to take a look at something similar, which is a sense of words. It was T. S. Eliot who said that poetry communicates before it is understood. By the same token I'm talking about that rather elusive ability we have - and can develop further - to experience the richness of language in a way that goes beyond simple comprehension of meaning or contextual understanding or a knowledge of the rules of grammar.

This kind of 'intuition' that helps us to appreciate words at a deep level is built into our brains. Furthermore, the appreciation is multi-sensory, and here we go back to the strange phenomenon of synaesthesia. We 'do language' with our whole bodies, which is why it now makes more sense to me when I hear the phrase 'to savour the words' as one might savour a fine wine or a delicate morsel.

By way of a brief and somewhat amusing diversion, look below at **Fig.11**. One of these shapes is called a *kitiki*. The other shape is called a *boobah*. Which is which? If you decided that the top shape is the boobah and the bottom shape is the kitiki then you're in the majority: around 95% of people, apparently, come to that conclusion. But how do we know? One suggestion is that we subconsciously link the round letter shapes of the word 'boobah' with the shape itself. Similarly with 'kitiki,' which is made up of thin spiky letters that we associate with the spikiness of the actual shape. Another idea is that to say the word 'boobah' our mouths must make rounded shapes, whereas to say 'kitiki' requires us to point the tongue and touch the back of the teeth. If you ask someone to explain why she feels boobah refers to the top shape, she's likely to mould the shape in the air with her hands. So here we have a combination of body movement, sound and shape

Fig.11: Kitiki and Boobah

contributing to our sense of what boobah and kitiki mean. Even though they are, technically speaking, nonsense words, we still make some kind of sense of them. This is in part the sense of words that I'm talking about, and which we can exploit to help give our language 'texture,' 'flavour,' 'roundedness' and 'depth.'

There is much fun to be had in playing with so-called nonsense words, even if you have no intention of following in the footsteps of Edward Lear or Lewis Carroll. Notice how you make sense of the following words . . .

* Glombous
* Snoodled
* Churdling
* Squeshy
* Gaart

Conventional knowledge of spelling and grammar plus association provides some meaning, but I wonder of you felt the temptation to hold the words in your hands, or if you savoured the sound of them as they formed in the mouth, or if visual images flickered across your mind's eye? And I wonder if even more elusive insights contributed to your knowingness?

Such an elegant sense of words also helps us as authors to select and combine words on a sentence-by-sentence basis as we write. What do you make of these two sentences?

a) Ellen held the treasure tightly, admiring its beauty and craft, as the coach rolled on into the unknown future and the roadway unravelled behind it.

b) Ellen held the object out in front of her, admiring its beauty and craftsmanship, as the coach sped through the night, on into the future, and the road disappeared behind it.

First of all, which sentence do you prefer? I'm not so much asking you to make a judgement using a coolly calculating 'editorial eye' as something rather more subjective - your sense of words. For me there's no doubt that sentence a) is the one I'd choose. Apart from its rhythm, the 'r' and 'l' add to the impression of the coach moving along the highway. Read aloud, that first sentence sounds and feels more pleasurable and satisfying. It's smoother, freer-flowing, easier, as oiled machinery is 'easier' than dry metal rubbing against dry metal. But what am I talking about? This is not critical analysis as such and certainly not literary appreciation. This is an attempt to explain how the sight and sound of the words in sentence a) have an effect on all of my senses. My sense of words, with its roots going deep into the creative subconscious, guides me as I decide on those words in the flow of composition, and verifies the correctness of my choice as I review the work.

So really I'm saying no more than that you bring to your writing a certain sensitivity as to the effect of words of your senses, and an attitude of playfulness as you engage with the language. In this way, I feel, you will more swiftly and surely develop your own individual voice.

Incidentally, this is the sense I made of the nonsense words we looked at earlier . . .

Something Goes By

It was a roiling night
of glombous reebs and grasting storm.
Barb owls huddled out the swirlwind's bite;
Decapedes in their hollows snoodled warm.

All through the low and high
of Shadowland the streams ran churdling
in the forest deeps. Moon's houring

sent out abalone light above the cloud hills hurdling,
while from the screamsome north -
the ice-teeth scouring
and breathly deathly cold came wreathing with a sigh.

Then
Something nudged and trudged aside the trees
and tramped the gladeland paths to squeshy mire;
made the seed-balloons pop and the opticus cry
as, in its thousand eyes,
the stars lay mirrored in the direful sky
and weepydrops crystalled red as vulcan fire.

Something comes this way
- goes by
something gaart and vast and sleez,
that sends the night mare riding
and the dawnflower fearfully hiding
as it passes, leaves its shadow
on the road to midnight seas.

24

50 Ideas to Boost Your Writing

Practice Piece 1 - The Walker

> Talking to yourself is the first sign of sanity.
> Listening to yourself is the second.
> *Phillipa Stephens*

I'll invite you now to review some of the ideas and techniques we've looked at so far. Our first practice piece is the picture below, *The Walker*. Attempt some or all of the following tasks.

* Imagine the scene with all of your senses. Turn up the colours. Be aware of the sounds. Step into the picture and experience the temperature. What odours can you smell? Touch three things and notice what they feel like. Become aware of a number of new and interesting details.

* Approach the walking man. Ask him three questions. What does his voice sound like as he replies?

* Decide (if his replies haven't told you) whether he is the hero, villain or a 'partner' in the drama - or perhaps a character serving another function. Use the 6x6 grid. Roll the dice twice. Wherever you land you will learn something more about this character.

* Construct a story line (see Fig. 3). Decide where along the narrative line this scene occurs. Use the Six Big Important Questions technique. Generate at least three questions under each category; three 'where' questions, three 'who' questions, etc. Use the coin flipping technique to obtain answers, or decide for yourself.

Fig.12: The Walker

★ Write a brief description of this scene...
   1. From the point of view of the walker.
   2. From a narrative overview.
   3. From the point of view of another unseen character who is antagonistic to the walking man.

★ If you are feeling ambitious (and have time to spare!) create a character pyramid for the walking man.

★ Consider how any themes you have identified as being important to your work generally might fit into a story built around the walking man. Does the picture suggest any further themes to you now?

★ Focus your attention on one part or detail of the picture. Use this to write a paragraph that opens this scene. Use the 'filmic' style of drawing out, panning, etc, to direct the reader's attention.

★ Using actual items or pictures cut from magazines, etc, placed within a circle, create a collage of what is going on in this character's mind right now. You may want to choose items at random and interpret them later.

★ Finally, go to the 6x6 grid again and roll the dice twice to choose an item that will tell you something about the walking man's destiny.

25

50 Ideas to Boost Your Writing

Collecting Motifs

> There is nothing so easy but that it becomes difficult when you do it reluctantly.
> *Terence*

I regard a motif as a constituent feature that helps to define and describe a larger domain. As we saw earlier, the thirty-six pictures featured in the grid we've been using are all motifs. Some of them are very particular to their domain - dragon, winged horse, two-headed dog. Others are more generally applicable across a range of domains: a chain or a forest, for example, might appear in any kind of story. Also, motifs might be used conventionally, sometimes to the point of cliché. We might expect the scene of a vampire's lair to include darkness, thunder and lightning, high winds, wolves howling, a token bat or two and perhaps an ear-piercing scream. But motifs can be used unconventionally, which often makes for an interesting creative challenge and can lead to some very original ideas. Imagine our vampire living in a cottage in a typically English village and you'll appreciate what I mean.

A technique that has helped my own writing to develop is called 'collecting motifs.' It simply involves making up a resource bank of details that can be put together subsequently to clarify and enrich the scenes within your story. Returning to the picture of the walking man, motifs that spring to mind immediately are:

- The lonely street.
- The hurrying figure.
- Rats in the alley.

- A discarded bottle.
- The tightly clutched bag.
- Mysterious pursuit.
- A sense of being followed.
- The scribbled note.

Perhaps others occur to you as you study the picture anew. Notice that these motifs are largely 'genre free.' Although they have been taken from a scene you might find in a Fantasy story or a drama set in the middle ages, most of them can be transposed into any kind of story. And therein lies their value. When you've collected a hundred motifs - and a walk down the High Street will garner dozens of them - you can put them together in endless combinations to suggest entire storylines, to pick out vivid descriptive details, to vary pace, suggest mood and atmosphere, and for many other purposes.

26

50 Ideas to Boost Your Writing

Position Statements and Fortune Cookie Language

> Art is not an end in itself,
> But a means of addressing humanity.
> M. P. Moussorgski

Two ideas similar to collecting motifs are 'position statements' and what I call 'fortune cookie language.' Position statements are most easily used in conjunction with storylines, either to help construct plots and subplots, to keep track of characters or as a handy way of summarising narratives. Simply annotate your storyline with statements like:

- The hero is unhappy.
- The villain arranges a trap.
- Two characters separate.
- A surprise helps someone.
- Her bravery is rewarded.
- The path divides.
- A disagreement leads to fear.
- Sheltering here causes problems.

Notice how position statements can easily be adapted from narrative sub-elements (see page 41), and how many lend themselves to further exploration through, perhaps, the Six Big Important Questions.

Fortune Cookie language amounts to the use of vague statements to prick the curiosity and encourage further investigation. See **Fig.13** below. Here, cross matching two such statements might suggest an intriguing situation that could be your doorway into a story. Or you might select a fortune cookie statement to kickstart the creative engine if the plot begins to wane.

	1	2	3	4	5
1	Consider your needs	Partnerships are likely	Look for signals	Time to separate	Be strong in a new way
2	Go into new areas	Choose carefully	Treasures are all round	Look to your defences	Protect yourself
3	Some object is important	Joy is arriving soon	Your plans bring rewards	Openings happen now	Fight for what you want
4	Now is a time of growth	Remove an obstacle	Go with the flow	Plans are upset	Important messages due
5	You are on a threshold	There is a breakthrough	All is still Be patient	Consider the whole thing	A secret and the unknown

Fig.13: Fortune Cookie Language

27

The Ten Sentence Game

*If I am not I,
who will be?*
Thoreau

There are several variations of this technique, which provides a basic 'scaffold' for the building of plots, characters and settings.

* Plot a story (perhaps using the storyline technique on page 22) using the following ten sentences in this order . . .

- *A shot rang out.*
- *He called her name.*
- *It was lost.*
- *And that was only the beginning.*
- *The door opened without a sound.*
- *It couldn't be true.*
- *Glass shattered nearby.*
- *There was a gasp of amazement.*
- *It missed by inches.*
- *They shook hands on the deal.*

* Take out five sentences at random. Shuffle the remaining five. Think of five new sentences and plot a story using the new batch of ten sentences.

* As above, but put a different emotional tone into the way you use the sentences. So, for example, use the ten sentences to

make a story that would be mildly humorous, or slightly chilling, or hilariously funny.

* Invent stories from different genres using the same ten sentences. So, how would the example sentences be used in a Science Fiction story? A Romantic Comedy? A Western?

* Deliberately set out to use either individual sentences or the whole batch with other activities presented in this book.

28

The Merlin Game

> It is our duty . . . to proceed
> as though the limits of our abilities
> do not exist.
> *Teilhard de Chardin*

The Merlin Game exploits the wizardry of our creative abilities by inviting us to wave the magic wand of the imagination in various ways. It is a focused and robust kind of brainstorming technique often used in the world of think tanks and big business, but employed for our purposes to develop the flexibility of our thinking with regard to creative fiction. You might use the Merlin Game in conjunction with the 6x6 grid or the ten-sentence game, or with other activities you've encountered in this book. Try it out too if you are suffering a 'block', or if you want to see if one good idea can stretch to several pieces of work.

In order to demonstrate the technique, let's refer to a story that we're all likely to know. Let's use the tale of Cinderella. First of all, take no longer than five minutes to write down all the motifs that come to mind - this would include characters, situations, objects, details of setting; in other words all of the bits and pieces, the constituent features, that make up the story as a whole.

Now what ideas spring to mind if you were to enlarge one or more motifs from the story? Just let your thoughts flow easily and value them all. Reject nothing. In the world of creative writing ideas are not right or wrong, good or bad, but more or less useful in the end. When you begin trying hard to think of new ideas, take a break.

Enlargement is one way to wave Merlin's wand. The other ways most commonly used are:

* Reduce
* Stretch
* Eliminate
* Substitute
* Reverse.

You can of course interpret 'stretch' and 'reverse' just as you like! If you go through the whole list using the motifs of Cinderella, you'll most likely end up with a number of intriguing new 'takes' on the story. The technique will be just as effective when it's applied to your own emerging work.

Incidentally, you might try the Merlin game as it applies to the *form* that the story can take. In considering *enlargement*, one group I worked with tackled motifs and came up with making Cinderella's feet swell, the prince having an inflated ego, the fairy godmother's magic snowballing out of control . . . Then one group member suggested *The Further Adventures of Cinderella*, in effect enlarging the concept beyond a single stand-alone story.

29

Dear Diary

> Where your talents and the
> needs of the world cross -
> There is your vocation.
> *Aristotle*

Diary writing has a long and respectable (and not so respectable) history. You may already keep a diary of course, but here are a few further ideas which you might find useful in boosting your creative writing more generally . . .

* Write an 'emotions diary,' exploring your inner landscape of thoughts and feelings without significant reference to what's going on in the outside world. Detaching what happens inside from external events highlights the fact that ultimately you are responsible for how you react, reflecting on the notion that responsibility can mean 'the ability we have to respond.'

* As an adjunct to the above, play the 'Fortunately - Unfortunately Game.' *Unfortunately my story was returned with a curt rejection today. Fortunately this gives me the opportunity to think about improving the work. Unfortunately I also want to get started on my next piece. Fortunately I can use my review of the earlier work to help prepare the next piece* . . . The value of this mental 'flipping of the coin' is that it develops the habit of thought of seeing two sides of a situation simultaneously. Furthermore, if you have something of a pessimistic streak the game puts a positive pressure on you to see the silver lining.

* If you are going through a rough patch with your writing, keep

a future diary of how good it feels to be over the tough times, looking forward now to more exciting endeavours and greater success.

* Keep a diary as though you were your story's main character. Or, if time permits, more than one of them.

* Keep a diary of your pseudonymous self (see also page 113). Even if you don't yet use a pseudonym, pretend you do and write as though you were that person/that aspect of your personality.

* Keep a 'serendipity diary' of the happy accidents that help to guide you along the road of your writing career, and of the weirdly wonderful way in which incidents seem to fit with your goals.

* Keep an 'agony aunt' (or uncle) diary, where you write entries as yourself-needing-help and replies from the part of you that can tap into your resources of wisdom and experience - essentially your creative centre.

30

Till Roll Writing

> Thousands of people have talent.
> The one and only thing that counts is -
> Do you have staying power?
> *Noel Coward*

If you have got into the habit of endlessly going back over your work adding bits here, altering bits there, never quite being satisfied that things are just right - then this simple technique might help to solve the problem . . . Take a till roll and begin writing. Let the paper strip curl up behind the pen, and don't look back until your writing session has finished.

The immediate value of tackling your work in this way is that you have to concentrate on what's happening now. Any temptation to review-as-you-write or cast a critical eye over the writing must be avoided, and soon you'll settle into a comfortable state of stream-of-consciousness writing, where the flow of composition follows the stream of thoughts passing through your mind.

Till roll writing is not the same as 'making it up as you go along,' although some writers indeed use the first idea that strikes them as a doorway into the world of the story and simply write it all out, learning as they go. Douglas Hill favours this strategy. I remember once when we were walking together in North London we passed a food shop selling falafal. 'Fallowfall,' Doug said immediately. I asked him what that meant. 'I don't know,' he replied, 'but I will soon.' His way of finding out would simply be to begin writing, letting ideas associate subconsciously and recording them in that raw state. After perhaps a hundred thousand words had been generated,

Doug would know all he needed to know about Fallowfall. The second drafting would carve the story out from that block of marble.

Although till roll writing can be used like this, my preferred strategy is to have mapped out the basic story first, even if that amounts to scattered notes in my notebook. Or I might have prepared a rough storyline, or created a 6x6 grid of motifs. I have found that the till roll writing flows more readily if I have done this basic organisation first.

If this little technique attracts you, then consider a few variations . . .

* Bifurcations. Return to a previous piece of till roll writing, perhaps a story that is no longer fresh in your mind. Begin reading from the start, and at each significant point think of an alternative scenario. 'A shot rang out - and he fell dead'. Or, 'A shot rang out, missing his head by an inch.' If you use the bifurcation (splitting into two) method throughout the story, you might have come up with insights for making it better or indeed for generating other plots.

* Parallel story. On two till rolls write the same story (or scene) from the point of view of two different characters.

* Use till roll writing as a group activity. Starting from the same opening sentence and/or basic plot, each group member writes his or her version of the tale. Discussing the differences can throw up many useful insights.

* Retrodiction. This is backwards-prediction. Start from the end of a till roll story and gradually work backwards, predicting what happens before the scene you're reading. This activity develops mental flexibility and checks the internal logical consistency of a plot.

31

50 Ideas to Boost Your Writing

Story Tree

> Rest satisfied with doing well,
> and let others talk of you as they will.
> *Pythagoras*

The story tree technique extends the idea of bifurcations. To make a story tree you will need a very large sheet of paper. Begin at the root of the story; with the initial idea or opening scene. Draw the trunk of the tree and add your starter sentence... *The engine sputtered and died. The car rolled to a halt on the lonely country road.* Now think of two 'what next?' ideas. A) *Inside the car Baxter chuckled, satisfied that his deception had worked.* B) *Inside the car Baxter sat rigid with fear. How would he escape now?*

On your sheet, draw two branches leading away from the trunk. Annotate the two branches with your two alternatives. Now select A) or B) - Let's say A). Draw two branches leading away from A) and at the end of each think of two alternatives...

A) *Inside the car Baxter chuckled, satisfied that his deception had worked.* A1) He slipped the gun from the glove compartment and waited for Smith to arrive. Or A2) Baxter's satisfaction was short-lived. A moment later the driver's door was pulled open and a shadowy figure reached towards him.

Now repeat with process with A1 and A2. If you hit a block go back down the tree to sentence B and strike off in another direction. You need not, of course, construct the tree on a sentence level like this. The branches could represent whole scenes, or even chapters if the novel is going to be substantial. By the same token, story trees often bear more fruit if you leave time between each 'growing session.' Doing too much at once can lead to fatigue and the tendency to try hard to think of another idea. Always give your mind time to process subconsciously.

How Do They Do It?

> The more I learn,
> the more I realise I don't know.
> *Albert Einstein*

If you want to be a writer then you have to be a reader. This is an obvious point, of course, but a vitally important one nevertheless. Taking note of how other authors achieve their effects allows us to model their techniques. This is not plagiarism, I hasten to add. To my mind plagiarism is the deliberate copying of another author's words: to realise that an admired author writes in the second person when describing dream sequences, for example, and using that technique yourself is different. Some years ago I wrote a few adult Horror novels under a pseudonym. I had noticed that other horror writers sometimes paid homage to classic tales of terror or to horror movies by making reference to them in their own stories - by using the same name for a street, for instance. I did the same in my books and felt happy that I had not plagiarised the writers of the stories I had referred to.

It's also very often true that in the process of developing our own 'voice' we mimic authors we admire. I have always loved the nature poetry of Ted Hughes, and throughout my teens my poems were (alas) pale copies of techniques that Hughes had used. In mimicking an author's chosen themes or style we become familiar with them. In a sense we become authorities in using them, and consider here the close link between authority and author. We become originators of our own ideas and voice out of the rich field of what other writers have done before us.

In taking note of how other writers do it, we must bear in mind - literally in fact - that there is a time to analyse and a time to compose. When I work with children on their writing I explain that there are three parts to making a story. The first part is the 'dreaming time.' This is the phase that most writers relish, when you are in that lovely relaxed mood simply noticing ideas and trains of thought as they drift across the mind's eye. This is the state of 'relaxed alertness' when the brain produces alpha waves and our attention swings away from the outside world and focuses on our own mental processes.

When we compose the work our brain state shifts. We are still aware of the imagery of the story - the film, as it were, is still running in our heads - but now we have to engage our critical faculties more as we reach for the right words in the flow of composition. Finally, with the work out there on paper (or on screen), we need to detach from it and look back with a critical eye asking ourselves, in essence -

* What changes do I need to make for this to be the best story I can make?
* What I have I learned by writing this that can make my next piece of work even better?

The process of envisioning - realising - analysing has been called the Disney Strategy, since it was noticed that Walt Disney went through these different mental phases in bringing his magical ideas to fruition.

In noticing how other writers do it and in practising those techniques we eventually assimilate them into our own working methods. As the poet Matsuo Basho said, Learn the rules well and then forget them. When we have absorbed the tricks of 'how it's done' they then emerge spontaneously as part of our own individual voice.

Thumbnails

> The moment when one truly commits oneself,
> then Providence moves too.
> *Goethe*

A thumbnail in computer-speak is a brief or miniature representation of a larger whole. The idea can be usefully transferred to one's writing practice. I use 127x76mm (5"x3") record cards for making thumbnails, which might be . . .

* Brief character descriptions with information abstracted from more detailed profiles (see page 57) or basic details which I add to as a character develops through a story.

* Sketchy ideas for short stories filed by theme, genre, or perhaps the order in which I intend to write them.

* Scene or chapter outlines for a novel. Using thumbnails in this way is, for me, the next step on from mapping the basic plot along a storyline (page 22). Chapter thumbnails help me to clarify my ideas and encourage me to work out the key scenes - there's no room to ramble on a thumbnail card!

* Key points in an article or longer piece of non-fiction work. Some years ago I wanted to write an educational book about thinking and creativity. I had masses of material drawn from workshops I'd run, hints and tips I'd picked up along the way and numerous other sources. Briefly recording each idea or reference on a thumbnail card meant I could then spread them out on the front room carpet and put them into a logical order. I don't think I

could have found a quicker and more effective way of getting the book ready to write.

* Story stimulus. If you belong to a writers' group you might consider collectively building up a thumbnail resource of workshop ideas. Or, as a workshop in itself, give each member of the group three blank file cards. On one card write a brief character description. On the second sketch out a setting, and on the third create an opening sentence. Mix and match the cards and notice the ideas that pop into mind.

34

Blurb It

> Either do not attempt at all,
> or go through with it
> *Ovid*

Look at the back cover of a paperback novel and notice how the blurb has been constructed. The writing of blurbs is an art in itself. It requires a clear understanding of the story, a knack for knowing what sells (and how) and insights into language that makes a swift emotional impact. Occasionally an editor will ask an author to suggest his own blurb - but it's worth writing them anyway as part of your working method. In the same way that a job applicant might be asked what special qualities he or she brings to the post, so an editor (or editor's reader) will be looking for an angle that gives your story the edge. By attempting to blurb your own work you will actively be checking for those same special qualities that make it, at least interesting and at best a must-have submission.

Blurb writing also encourages brevity and clarity. When submitting longer pieces of work you might prefer to (or be asked to) send an outline and a few sample chapters rather than the whole manuscript. If you have blurbed the work you can incorporate those crisp, clear sentences into your covering letter - but leaving out 'His/Her latest bestseller'!

35

50 Ideas to Boost Your Writing

Be Somebody (Else)

> Who does not tire achieves.
> *Spanish Proverb*

I have used three pseudonyms so far in my writing career. The most important came about when I thought I'd try my hand at writing adult Horror fiction. I wanted the book to be very violent with lots of graphic, explicit horror. The main reason for this was that I was going through a difficult patch in my life and I was filled with anger. I knew that violent, angry writing would be a safe, creative and therapeutic way of expressing my rage. I had a plot that I was pleased with, I'd made sufficient notes and so I sat down to write. . . And struggled and battled with the book, and after thirty pages gave up in despair. Why, I asked myself, couldn't I bring myself to create this stuff?

The answer came to me shortly afterwards in a true moment of illumination. I didn't want my work colleagues or my Mum to know I'd done it! In the same way that we know when a name we've just remembered is the *right* name, so I was in no doubt that I'd hit upon the true reason for my creative block. The solution also suggested itself effortlessly - write the adult Horror under a pseudonym.

I decided that, rather than try to make up a suitable-sounding name I'd let the law of serendipity help me. I was a schoolteacher at the time and on this one of many occasions I had piles of marking in front of me. I lifted some of the books off the pile and glanced at the first name of the pupil whose book I'd uncovered. *Ben.* A good strong name, I thought; just right. I split the pile again and glanced at the surname revealed. *Leech*. It was perfect. And so was born Ben Leech whose career so far has spanned three novels and half a dozen short stories.

What I found even more intriguing than the way the name appeared by chance was the fact that Ben could write the horror more easily and successfully than could Steve Bowkett. I came to realise that Ben represented an aspect of my personality that needed to express itself for my overall wellbeing. Letting Ben have his say - as he wanted to say it - did me a power of good. By the time I'd finished my first Ben Leech novel my anger was out and no-one got hurt except some of the characters in the book.

A pseudonym, then, can be a very useful device for psychological reasons and, indeed, for commercial ones. A number of authors write different kinds of books under different names. When this works it allows publishers to clearly associate an author with a particular genre, while allowing that author to strike out in different directions without flooding the market with her work or 'blurring the marketing categories' that the publishers most likely want to maintain.

My second pseudonym came into existence when I was asked to write a children's romantic novel as part of a new series. The target audience was girls of 10 to 12 years old. I duly wrote the book and titled it *The Wishing Star*. A week later my editor rang to say she liked the story but I'd have to change the name. I told her that I thought *The Wishing Star* was a pretty good title. 'No, no,' she added, 'I want you to change your *name*.' And she went on to explain that the marketing department had decided that 10 to 12-year-old girls were more likely to buy romantic fiction written by women, so I had to invent a female pseudonym for myself. I should let you know that my first names are Philip and Stephen, and so shortly afterwards Philippa Stephens emerged in all her feminine elegance.

I'm still waiting for Philippa to be invited to speak at the Romantic Novelists' Association . . .

Finally, to complete my trilogy of pseudonyms, I invented Len Beech. Some years ago I co-wrote a novel with an author whose style and vision of the book were very different from my own. The work had been commissioned and the contracts signed, so I couldn't back out, besides which I wanted to feel that I had some integrity left. So I persevered, but increasingly came to see that the book was not working. My sections read like bits bolted on to the main plot. Writing as Len allowed me to limp past the finishing line and fulfil my obligations, but it was he, I'm sorry to say, who bore the brunt of the poor reviews that followed the book's publication.

36

The Journeyman

> It does not matter how slowly you go,
> as long as you do not stop.
> *Confucius*

I write because, at a very deep level, writing gives me a sense of purpose and fulfilment. But I never want to be precious about my work or to stand haughtily on matters of artistic principle. This is part of the attitude towards authorship I alluded to in the introduction; the question of how we regard ourselves as authors.

Early on in any writing career it's tempting to acquiesce to every editorial suggestion, be it good advice, whim or egotistical insistence, because otherwise we fear the plug would be pulled and we'd lose the chance of publication. This was exactly the position in which I found myself, though as time went on I came to realise that the best editors worked creatively with the author to make the book as good as it could be, within a relationship of mutual respect. Less experienced or less sensitive editors, however, can be prickly, critical, obstructive and on occasions downright dismissive. In one instance, because I kept challenging the editor's endless negative feedback on my work, she reserved her right to cancel the contract and demanded the advance be returned.

Hopefully you'll work with lots of editors - but what will your attitude be as a writer? I can't of course tell you how to do it but only how I do it. My core principles to authorship are . . .

* The principle of utilisation. Whatever I experience in my writing career, pleasant or unpleasant, I endeavour to use positively to

allow me to continue towards my fixed goal of making a life out of my writing.

* The principle of diversification. For my first six years as a published author I was concentrating on writing Science Fiction and Fantasy stories for boys of about 10-12 years old. Then someone uttered to me the single wisest word of authorial advice I've ever heard. *Diversify.* That simple suggestion, to open my wings and fly, has led to some modest success in half a dozen different fields of writing. These days I am always actively looking for fresh fields to explore. The pleasure of looking for the new whilst enjoying the old is, I'm sure you'll appreciate, immense.

* The principle of recycling. In the world of writing nothing is ever wasted. Ideas that didn't work are never thrown away. I'll go back to them, sometimes years later, and see what I can make of them now. By the same token, if I have a good idea I'll try to turn it into more than one piece of work: an idea I use in a novel might also work up into a short story, and could supply the theme for a poem as well.

* All of these contribute to the principle of the journeyman. I love writing SF, Fantasy and Horror, but if I'm asked to write a teenage romance novel I'll consider it as a creative challenge. And if I accept the challenge, I'll do my level best to rise to it.

37

Countdown to a Story

> We are what we repeatedly do.
> *Aristotle*

I have endeavoured to show you some strategies and techniques that have helped me to have ideas, organise them and compose them - all underpinned by the creative attitude.

In this last segment of *50 Ideas to Boost Your Writing* I'd like to extend that creativity into the reviewing phase of preparing work for submission and beyond when editorial responses arrive at your door (or do not, as the case may be!). You might find the following checklist useful to making a general review of the material . . .

20) Are my themes clear to me? To my readers?
19) Have I decided upon a genre? Why do I choose to write in this field?
18) How far has the 'territory' of my story been explored before? How? By whom? With what results?
17) Am I bringing something fresh to this field? What? How?
16) Am I using the motifs of the genre deliberately, constructively, effectively?
15) Do I know enough about my characters? Are they 'in-formed' and clear in my mind?
14) Is the storyline mapped out clearly?
13) Have I considered variations, twists and alternatives within this overall plan?

12) Do I have an idea of the extent of this piece of work? Have I settled on a plan-of-work in terms of when and where, how long and how often I'll write?
11) Does my overall plan incorporate a chapter and/or scene breakdown? If not, will it help me to have one?
10) Are the themes, genre, characters, storyline and breakdown congruent - do they fit well together?
9) Are the background and settings for the story clear and appropriate?
8) Do I have at least a working title?
7) Whose point of view will the narrative take? Would an alternative point of view be more appropriate, effective, original?
6) How do I feel as I prepare to begin this work? Am I confident, excited, filled with a creative buzz? (If not, what must I now do to achieve that resourceful state?).
6) Do I have a first scene/paragraph/sentence in mind?
4) Have a considered a more powerful way of beginning the tale?
3) Have I organised my working time so that I can write without distractions?
2) Is there anything else I need to attend to before I begin?
1) Do I have a hot cup of tea nearby?

Yes? Then begin.

I also use a 'count up from a story' once I have completed it (the first draft anyway).

1) Am I broadly happy with the outcome?
2) Am I especially satisfied with particular passages?
3) Do I know why I am pleased with them?

4) Am I particularly dissatisfied with any parts of this story?
5) Do I know how to fix them?
6) Can I use anything from this story in any future projects?
7) Can I 'repackage' the story in some other way? Could it generate a sequel?
8) What have I learned about writing by making this story?
9) What have I learned about myself by writing this story?
10) Do I know how to prepare this story for submission?
11) Have I researched the market so I know where to send it?
12) Do I know how to count down towards my next project?

38

A Sense of Audience

> He that seeks finds.
> *Spanish Proverb*

Yes, I know you may be thinking 'Why didn't he mention this earlier?' Surely writers need to know whom they are writing for before they begin? Of course that's true, and I'm assuming that you will already have made necessary decisions in this area. On the other hand, I suggest that if you begin to worry about 'hitting a target audience' or 'slotting into the market' the balance of your concern has tipped towards the negative and you are in danger of inhibiting your creativity and limiting the freshness and effectiveness of what you want to say.

For many years, before I ever entertained the notion of becoming a 'real live author' I simply *wrote to please myself*, and I still regard this as a fundamental principle of keeping my work alive. We write most naturally and powerfully, most originally, when we are inspired. When I'm describing a scene or a character I must be alive in and to that world, sometimes to the point where I lose myself there and become unaware that I'm sitting at my computer, in my house, along this street, in this town. When I am alive in this way the world I express shares that life, and that's when I produce my best work.

Inspiration also means 'to breathe forth,' which links directly with the point that's just been made. Inspired writing is a breath of fresh air. It inspires others, evoking a sense of shared life and experience. I think that to write in this spirit is essentially an unselfconscious act, and that if we become too hung up on writing to please others we can dull that vital energy.

As I say these things I realise I'm talking to some extent about the envisioning of the world of the story and the exuberant flow of first-draft composition. What comes out may be alive but untidy, imprecise, or too much the product of spontaneous thinking. Obviously we must look back at the work and be as sure as we can that the words say what we intended them to say. The whole process of story making utilises the powers of the whole mind, from the sometimes-unfocused cascade of ideas rising from the subconscious, to the cool, critical-analytical logic of our conscious selves. With this in mind (as it were) I find it useful to consider the *Four 'I's* . . .

* Imagination. Our ability to construct mental impressions at will, to evoke the world of the story.

* Immersion. Our ability to 'jump into' the world we evoke, to experience life there - the life of the place itself and of the characters who populate it.

* Intuition. Our ability to recognise our own 'inner tuitions,' that subtle but powerful sense of rightness in expressing the worlds we create through language. In other words, the power we have to know when a story is working.

* Intellectual Skills. Our ability to make word-by-word decisions as we write, and then to detach and look back coolly and critically at the whole work in order to put the finishing touches to the project.

*

In short, at the outset my audience is myself. As you know, I also like to write within certain genres for certain age groups - I relish writing fantasy stories for 10-13 year-olds, for instance. To help keep my mind focused on that audience I might make use of character types (see page 53), using a boy like Tony or a girl like Eleanor as the 'archetypal child' to whom I am telling the story. Having an impression of that person in mind as I write helps me to say the right things in the right way. You can, of course, have a real child in mind: many successful and popular children's stories were written for the author's children or grandchildren. In that case you also have the benefit of immediate - and usually devastatingly honest - feedback!

Although, as I have said earlier, I am a 'journeyman,' accepting whatever authorial challenge comes my way if it interests me at all, I am very disinclined to chase the market or to bow unthinkingly to editorial opinion. I write children's fantasy because I love it, not because that genre is currently very popular. If the fantasy fad fizzled out and, say, children's Western stories surged on to the bookshelves, I'd still write Fantasy. If, by some chance, an idea occurred to me for an innovative Western novel, I might then give it some sustained but cautious thought.

A good editor is one who believes in your work and will do all she can to help make it the best book it can be. I guess it comes down to one's own judgement in deciding when constructive advice becomes naïve interference, limiting criticism or ego-led 'creative input.' I have more to say about editors later, but now let me lay a few basic cards on the table.

* The energy I put into editorial advice is in proportion to the commitment that editor/publisher has already made to the project. If I've already signed a contract and consider the editor's comments to be reasonable, I'll do my best to comply. If an editor suggests swingeing changes and then mentions she'd be prepared to look at the book again, I almost never commit to that extra work.
* If an editor makes positive noises (count the number of times

the word 'exciting' appears) about an outline, synopsis or sample chapters of a book I've not yet written, making no commitment at that stage, but wants changes and then to see the completed work, I will not make those changes. It's all too easy to invest months writing the book her way, for her then to reject it outright. This has happened to me before. You then either have to rewrite it *your* way, or send it off as-is and be prepared for the next editor in line to suggest *further* changes based on her preferences. This can result in an endless cycle of frustration and disappointment.

* I don't make changes just on the basis of negative editorial feedback. If several editors all make the same critical observations, then I'll look at the work again. In the case of my first Ben Leech novel, the first editor I sent it to felt that the story was trite and derivative, the characters unconvincing and the sex and violence in the plot wholly gratuitous. Bruised, but otherwise uninjured, I sent it to a second publisher whose Horror editor loved the originality of the plot, felt the characters had sufficient depth and variety and agreed that the graphic sex and violence were in keeping with the themes of the story and with the genre overall. That publisher not only bought the book but also contracted for another two.

My position then, is that I feel the need to be true to myself. If I am not independent in my judgement (without being closed to good advice), then I will be blown about on the winds of others' opinions. A good editor will always listen to an author's case for keeping things as they are. To have an argument at all about why you've said something in that way proves that you have written deliberately and with foresight, to the best of your ability.

However, if you are happy to go along with every editorial suggestion that comes your way, then bear in mind the advice that Arthur C. Clarke once gave in the event of being abducted by aliens ... Be very polite, and be prepared for a long journey.

Casting a Critical Eye

> Great things are not done by impulse.
> *Vincent Van Gogh*

I think that writers know when they've done a good piece of work: we experience a welling up of those feelings of pleasure, satisfaction, contentment (perhaps spiced a little with pride), which reassure us of our achievement. I have always found it to be strange, therefore, when work that I feel I've done well is returned dismissively or with negative commentary - similarly when work that I know is not my best is accepted. However, it is obviously in our own interests to maximise the chances of the manuscript being noticed on the slush pile, given an initial reading and, hopefully, making a good impression.

Before I'm ready to send a manuscript I review it twice. Firstly I make a general review which looks at these four areas . . .

1) Conventions of Genre and Form. How correctly and elegantly have I used the motifs of the genre? I would expect to use them conventionally, but have I been deliberately unconventional in a way that will give the work freshness and added punch? Similarly I need to be sure that the form the work takes adds to its clarity. Conventionally a piece of prose fiction will follow the expected structure of a narrative, with sentences logically linked that build into paragraphs and scenes and, in longer stories, into chapters. I like to balance dialogue and description, vary the pace, control mood and atmosphere - in short all of the aspects that earmark competent writing. But again, have I been deliberately unconventional, and why? If

unconventionality is part of your artistic purpose then it can make your work stand out. If it's done just to be different or outrageous, then it's not likely to get past the first hurdles.

2) Emotional Responses. Most writers know the advice 'show, don't tell.' Stories at their best are experiences, where the reader is immersed in the world of the author's creation. The mood and atmosphere should be felt. We should find ourselves reacting emotionally to the characters. Because it's my story, I know how I should feel as I read it through. But what have I done to create the intended responses in my readers?

3) Vivid Particularities. We looked at these earlier - details in the work that create a striking visual impression and make a strong emotional impact. Study other writers. Which sentences stand out? How did the author achieve that effect? Sprinkling your writing with vivid particularities will help to give it that power and individuality we all strive towards.

4) Technical Aspects. Writing that is consistently accurate in a technical sense (without being pedantic or over-formal, of course) creates a favourable impression. Work that is riddled with errors creates an impression of ignorance or laziness, or both. The phrases 'to publish' and 'to make public' are closely linked. When a piece of writing leaves your study you are making it public. It represents you. It speaks for you and about you. Taking care over small technical details reflects your desire to maintain high standards.

Another technique I use is called 'writer's pie.' Draw a circle and divide it into six or eight segments. Associate each segment with some aspect of your work. Such an aspect might be rather broad such as 'degree of humour' or narrow like 'correct use of apostrophes'. Read your work for pleasure and when you've finished, make a mark in each slice of the pie, following the general rule that the closer to the edge you make the mark, the more successfully you feel you've dealt with that aspect.

This provides you with something of an overview. Now take one aspect of the work - one slice of the pie - and ask yourself, 'What clues can I notice which led me to make the mark *just there?*' This stimulates a more thorough and more evidence based review which focuses your attention more finely. Keep your writer's pies over the course of months and compare the same aspects occasionally. You may well be delighted to find how far you've improved.

40

The Soul of Style

> Lucidity is the soul of style.
> *Hillaire Belloc*

Have you heard the story of the ant and the centipede? One day an ant spied a centipede walking along the path and was struck with wonder and admiration at the marvellous elegance and co-ordination of the centipede's legs. The ant called to the centipede and complimented him on the grace and beauty of his walking style. 'But how do you do it?' the ant was interested to know. 'I haven't really ever given it any thought,' replied the centipede. 'But now let me see . . .' The centipede considered the matter carefully and at last came up with a number of rules governing his wonderful ability to walk. These he explained in great detail to the ant, who listened, entranced. 'Well,' said the ant finally, 'I am amazed. Thank you so much for troubling to tell me. Now I must be getting home, I have so much to do!' And with that he scurried away. 'Indeed,' said the centipede, 'I have lots to do as well and should also hurry home. Now, rule one . . .'

There is an argument for over-analysing one's work. It has been wisely said that a book is never really finished but only ever abandoned. The law of diminishing returns can operate to the extent that the effort involved in picking away at tiny details becomes disproportionate to any beneficial effects achieved.

There is also the point to be made that *trying hard* to write well, writing in a state of constant self-consciousness as to style or individual 'voice' reduces the whole process to something forced and mechanical, taking away the spontaneity and human heart of the work.

There is of course nothing wrong with reflecting on the particular qualities that make the writing one's own, but my suggestion here is that ultimately the soul of style can be safely left to flourish by itself, without too much interference from the conscious analytical mind. As the philosopher Alan Watts once said about life, regard it as a mystery to be enjoyed rather than a puzzle to be solved.

41

Practice Piece 2: *Going Along for the Ride*

> Whether you think you can or you can't -
> You are right.
> *Henry Ford*

It's impossible for me to know how far you have walked along the road to mastery as far as your writing is concerned. Perhaps you've found my ideas and suggestions basic and naïve or possibly, some of them at least, useful revelations. Do feel free to skip this segment if you're not minded (or not in the mood) to do some revision.

Read the short story below and consider the points that follow.

Going Along For The Ride

Rocks McGee was a sinner. He knew it. We all knew it. He was in fact the biggest sinner in New York State. I'm tellin' you there was evil in that man's mind. But did it trouble him? You bet your life it didn't trouble him a cent. In fact he used to smile when he recalled all the nasty things he'd done and he'd say to me when I mentioned it to him, "Hal," he'd say - Hal being my name, like - "Hal, I've been grinnin' all my born days. It's the way I look at life, see. When I was five I stole a handful o' toffees from Ma Jacobs' sweet shop, and I grinned when she caught me. Last month we had that shootout with the Franz Grayson mob down at the docks and the rat winged me and it hurt like hell - and I grinned in that guy's face to show him I ain't never gonna bow down to fear and pain. You get my meanin' Hal?"

I got his meaning all right and I nodded kind of nervously. And Rocks's grin broke into a beaming smile and he started to laugh. He laughed and laughed like the devil was in him, tickling his ribs from the inside. Man, I just shivered. I never saw anybody get so much pleasure outa bein' bad!

Mention of the Grayson gang brings me back to the reason why I'm talkin' to ya. It was a messy business all right, because although we gave them a good hiding a lot of innocent folks got caught up in it too, and there were some regrettable injuries. That meant the heat was on even more. Just about every cop in town was lookin' for us after that and so Rocks decided that the wisest thing was for us to go on the lam.

In short, we ran.

But after a month of that we got tired of dusty roads and cheap motels and bad food and no fun. Why, even Rocks's grin was sagging a little at the edges. So one day he gathers us round - the whole bunch of us around a table in a second-rate eatery in the middle of nowhere; that's me (Hal the Blade), Lil Silk, Bubbles and The Shade - and he says to us, "Guys," he says, "I'm sick o' this runnin' and hidin' and I reckon it's time we got us a whole mess o' fun!"

And his grin comes on like a two-bar electric fire and I see the blue glint in his left eye (his right eye being made of glass).

"You plannin' a caper, Rocks?" asks Lil, that being the question on every one of our minds and the most intelligent thing she's said all week.

"Now Lil," Rocks says in his most reasonable tone - meaning when he's at his most dangerous. "Now Lil," he says, "you know me. When the heat's on we gotta keep cool, right?"

We all laughed a bit at that because Rocks liked us to appreciate his little jokes.

"So no, no caper. At least nothin' to worry you too much."

And then he takes out this wad of foldin' green and flickers the moolah in front of our noses and boy, them greenbacks smell as sweet as strawberries to me.

"Like I says," he says, "we're gonna have some fun!"

"Fun." The Shade says it like he's been invited to his own funeral, because if there's one thing that fella can't abide it's fun.

But Rocks is on the up and he's tellin' us about this crazy funfair he read about on a leaflet that blew under the door to his room on a cold October wind. "Woke me up," he says, "right on the dot of midnight."

"Oooo, creepy," squeals Lil and uses that as an excuse to cuddle up to Rocks and sniff that money some more.

He waves the leaflet at us and it smells of fireworks and autumn leaves. "I reckon we've worked hard this year what with taking down the Grayson Gang and lammin' out of the Big Apple and all, so I thought it was time for me to give you a treat. So, you coming along for the ride?"

"You mean you're paying, honey?" says Lil all gooey-eyed and flashy-lashed and lipsticky-smiley.

And Rocks grins and nods - and I grin too because I know from experience that when Rocks McGee treats he treats BIG.

*

It was like the whole universe was a blaze of lights; the reds and yellows, the blues and purples and greens all flashed and sparkled, whooshed and spun around us. I hadn't been to a fairground in years and this one took my breath away.

It was way out in the desert, and when it first came up out of the boiling sea of hot air as we drove there the following afternoon it looked like one of them mirages, all shimmery and vague. But as we got closer the sun was going down beyond the red Arizona hills and the sky turned purple and the desert started to cool: the fairground complex solidified and the strains of a hurdy-gurdy came wafting across the orange sands out of the far distance. By the time we parked up the sky was black and powdered with stars and a big full moon was hanging in a nearby joshua tree with a surprised look on its round white face.

"OK . . . kids. . . ," Rocks said between puffing a corona that was as thick as Lil's ankle. "What's everyone . . . want to do?"

"Oh what about the Tunnel of Love?" cooed Bubbles, who'd always had eyes for The Shade. The Shade tried to look properly tough and mean, but I saw him give a little frightened shake of his head when Rocks glanced over.

"Personally I'd go for the shooting gallery," The Shade said with a touch of menace. I quite fancied the dodgems, while I knew Rocks had a weakness for the carousel. In the end we went on all of these and more, and for the next couple of hours wandered about wherever the soft desert breeze would take us. We looked at the lightshows with our mouths open like kids - and kept them open to eat hotdogs and toffee apples and great plumes of candyfloss that felt like you were eating sugarcoated clouds. We laughed and joked and fooled around and it was as though we had gone back to our days of innocence when the whole of life had been like this. It put a sweet sharp pain in my heart that made me want to cry.

For a time, once that thought had passed, my mind was diverted by trips on the Waltzer and the Whirler and the Highdiver that lifted us so high and dropped us so fast that Lil's scream was left behind and caught up with us ten seconds later. The fun washed through us and wrung us out like old dishcloths until we dragged ourselves to a coffee stand to catch our breath.

"OK," said Rocks once we had finished our coffee (except for Lil who left hers. She looked a little green). "Something less energetic I think."

"The Tunnel of Love?" wondered Bubbles. She batted her eyelashes at The Shade and the breeze nearly blew his hat off.

"Um, well, no . . ." Rocks sounded kind of strange, as though he was keeping something from us. "I was looking forward to going on the ghost train."

He said it in a definite kind of way, with a tone that warned against arguments.

"I mean, you gals can close your eyes if you like - although there'll be plenty o' chances for a cuddle, eh Bubbles? Eh Lil?"

Well that was the girls sorted out. The Shade went wherever Rocks went, close as a shadow (which is why he was called The Shade). Rocks looked at me.

"Sure, suits me," I chirped up, still not liking the way the light glinted slyly in his one good eye.

Anyway, we made our way across the complex until we found the ghost train. It was pretty much hidden away behind a Hall of Mirrors and a Kaleidoscope Show; sort of tucked back out of sight in a little patch of gloom where most folks wouldn't bother to go. And unlike the other attractions the ghost train wasn't all lit up. Just the opposite in fact. Except for a dim yellow bulb in the pay-booth the whole place was draped in darkness.

"All part of the atmosphere I guess," Lil said nervously.

Man, was I spooked already!

Rocks walked over to pay and we caught sight of the guy in the booth. I thought he was dead. He was the palest, thinnest, driest looking dude I ever set eyes on. He was slumped back in his chair with his eyes closed and he didn't look to be breathing at all.

"Hey, let's blow," I said. "It's a stiff. I don't care to take the rap for this one!"

"Quit flappin' yer gums," Rocks replied, more aggressively than he needed to. He tapped the edge of a dime on the counter and the ticket seller's eyes opened slowly. It was like a scene from The Mummy Awakes.

"Five," Rocks said. "Adults. Please."

The ticket seller's lips parted like two dry leaves curling back and he smiled. Believe me, I've seen some hoods in my time but this smile made me tremble with the evil it suggested. Rocks took out another cigar and nearly dropped it. He cut the end and puffed out big billows of smoke, making like the big man while the ticket seller sorted out his change and wound out five tabs of soft yellow paper from his machine, then pushed them across without a word.

Rocks nodded and led us to a rickety old wooden carriage waiting there all by itself. Just ahead were the two big swing doors to the entrance of the ride. They were shaped like giant coffin lids.

"I'm not so sure about this," Lil gulped. She looked at the doors and then at Rocks and back to the doors again. " Maybe I'll just wait it out while you guys - "

There was a bang and a lurch and a squeak of rusty wheels and we were off. We barged through the coffin lid doors and sailed on into a vast, cool musty smelling darkness.

For long, long moments there was only the dry whispering wind and the feeling that we were swirling away from the world we knew and into some other place that wasn't quite as nice. Rocks and Lil sat together at the front, with Lil clutching the boss's coat sleeve for all she was worth. Bubbles and The Shade sat immediately in front of me. I shrank down behind them and picked away at the peeling black paint of the carriage - And holy moly did I get a shock! It came away in patches like human skin, and the wood seeped a dark liquid that I didn't care to examine too closely.

I might have said something about it, but then the horror show began. Plastic skeletons dropped from the ceiling. Rubber bats swooped by my face. Papier mache masks loomed out of the darkness and the air was filled with shrieks and howls and crazy laughter coming from clapped-out speakers hidden behind cardboard headstones. Heck, it wasn't so bad, I even started to like it until . . .

We sailed into a pale sea of mist and suddenly I realised that I couldn't hear the rattle of the car's wheels on the rails any more. But we were still moving, sort of drifting in a limboland between here and there.

"Rocks," I said, scared enough to voice my growing concern, "what's going on Boss? Where are we?"

"Listen up," Rocks came back at me - at all of us. "Don't you start whinin' now, not when I've paid so much for this journey. You guys were fed up of running, right? You was tired of worrying that at any time a cop might jump out from around some corner and feel ya collar. You wanted fun, yeah? And some freedom. And a break from the cares of the world . . . Well ya got it, so quit yappin' and wait and see what ol' Rocks has arranged for your entertainment. . ."

Actually, that's all we could do.

The carriage was moving more quickly; at least that was the sensation inside. I could feel the wind whipping by me and it was a warm wind too, but the warmth of a bonfire rather than the desert. Then up ahead, at a tremendous distance, I saw a light appear. I knew that marked the end of my journey. And the pang in my heart came back with a vengeance - that awful regret of the loss of childhood days and the things I'd done since. All the wrong that lay rotting inside me. Well, I told myself, what else could I expect?

The speed of the car was so great now that I couldn't summon breath to call out, and I had to hang on for grim death to stay in my seat. Up ahead the red glow was brighter and I caught the first stink of sulphur in the air. I wanted to whisper a few words to all the people I'd hurt and I wanted their forgiveness and comfort but it was far too late for that.

Now the darkness was shredding aside like charred paper and the huge galleries of fire and light were opening up around me. Who could I blame but myself? I'd hitched myself to Rocks and gone along for the ride, and now I had no choice in my destination.

Maybe Rocks had read my thoughts or something, for at that moment he looked round and there was devilment in his eyes - in both of them.

And he was grinning.

*

★ What are your first impressions of the story?

★ What, if anything, did you particularly like about the tale? What didn't you like?

★ What are the themes of the story?

★ What genre would you say it fits into?

★ What age range do you suppose the story was written for? How do you envisage the 'archetypal reader' of this tale?

★ What emotional responses do you feel the author was trying to evoke in the reader? How far do you judge that he succeeded?

★ How did the author attempt to sketch out the characters in the story? How far do you think he succeeded?

* Do you notice any particular points of style that characterise the story?
* Would you do anything to improve this tale?
* Write a very brief blurb for the story.

42

Into the Wild Blue Yonder

> Be an opener of doors.
> *Ralph Waldo Emerson*

The time will come - if it has not done so already - when you submit your work to an agent or publisher for consideration. Many books on the craft of writing have dealt with this topic so I don't want to spend much time going over that ground here. If I may, however, I'd like to mention a few points that I bear in mind when I send my work into the wild blue yonder.

★ Use the *Writers' & Artists' Yearbook*, or ring up the publishing house, to find out the name of the commissioning editor for the kind of work you're submitting. Address the parcel to him/her personally.

★ Make sure the manuscript is immaculately presented. Include a title page and a very brief covering letter to the effect - 'I enclose a manuscript for a (Fantasy/Horror story for 10-12 year-olds) and would very much appreciate you giving it your consideration.' If you have a 'track record' of previously published work, competition wins, etc, you can include that on a separate sheet. Include return postage, or you can specify that the work is a disposable copy, in which case include an SAE for a letter of reply.

★ Be patient, but don't wait forever for an editor to respond. My own method is to wait three months. If the manuscript has not been returned or any reply made, I'll send a polite letter wondering if the manuscript, which I posted on such-and-such-a-date, has been received. If I hear nothing after another two months, I send a slightly pricklier letter wondering if the editor has had time to look at the manuscript which I posted on such-and-such-a-date. If I hear nothing after a further month I ask for my manuscript to be returned. Usually, of course, the book comes back more swiftly than that, but on the other hand one doesn't want to grow old and die waiting for a response by one editor among hundreds.

* Never pester the editor. Phonecalls or emails asking if/when your book will be considered are likely to meet with a chilly response.

* Even if a manuscript is rejected, don't be put off submitting other work to that editor. Eventually your name will become known. My first editor returned a book I'd sent with a letter saying, 'I don't want to publish this, but I quite like what you're doing. Come and see me.' That led to my first contract, although I had to pay my own train fare down. . . Also bear in mind that editors quite often move on. A year or two down the line and someone else, who may look on your work quite differently, might be sitting at that desk.

* Once you've submitted a piece of work, don't wait by the letter-box. Forget it and get on with your next project.

* You should not send the same piece of work to more than one editor at a time (Frustrating, I know). Simultaneous submissions are frowned upon. But by all means keep your manuscripts circulating. In my early days I had five or six children's novels doing the rounds. I made myself a grid with the titles of the novels along the top and target publishers down the left-hand side. I used paper tabs to help me keep track of which book I'd sent where, and on which date.

* *Always* have other ideas in development. If an editor likes your work she will most probably ask you what other stories you've written, or will be writing. Despite tales of debut novels attracting huge advances, in the overwhelming number of cases a first novel won't recoup its costs. Publishers would be looking to earn their investment back over two, three or more books. This does not necessarily apply to 'jobbing' work, where a publisher, say, offers you a flat fee for a one-off project. Even so, as a writer your soul *needs* to be busy on the next story.

43

50 Ideas to Boost Your Writing

Agents and Etiquette

> A yes-man stoops to concur
> *Anonymous graffito*

I know authors who swear by their agents (sometimes at them) and other authors who feel that they are a waste of time. My own feelings are mixed. The best agents, like the best editors, believe in your work and will do all they can to see it succeed. Good agents will actively promote your projects, keep you informed of publishers' projects that might suit you, negotiate better deals (thereby effectively earning their percentage from the publisher, not you), offer cogent guidance and advice on improving your work and act as an agony aunt (or uncle) and a stout shoulder to cry on. I've never had an agent who has done all that for me. Bad agents will simply pass your manuscripts on to a publisher and, if you meet with some success, charge their percentage - and expect you to pay their VAT on top.

My opinion is that an agent's letter accompanying a manuscript carries some weight. The editor can assume that the work has been looked at and approved by a professional eye. Having said that, good editors can and should judge manuscripts for themselves - the work speaks with its own voice and its quality (and marketability) will shine through. Not having an agent need not prevent you from actively submitting your projects: I've met many people who feel that the book won't stand a chance otherwise, but I don't believe that this is the case. You can also submit a book simultaneously to a publisher and an agent, although make it clear that you're doing this. When you send work to an agent, do so to the same standard as when you submit work to an editor. If an agent is interested in you (and I mean 'you,' over and above a manuscript) she'll ask to meet you and will want to know about your further ideas. Always have some in mind. In days gone by authors and agents often made a verbal agreement to work with one another, but now the common practice is to enter into a written contract. If you reach this point read the document carefully and, if necessary, seek professional advice about exactly what it means. Agents, most likely, are not going to fleece you, but common sense says study the small print.

44

Nightmare Tales

> Always bear in mind that your own resolution to succeed is more important than any other thing.
> *Abraham Lincoln*

Somebody once told me that you know you're past it when you quite like the idea of being a Grumpy Old Man. I don't believe it of course, because it means that I've been one since I was about twenty-five years old. After all these years in the business I've met with some success and also had some nightmare rides. Many people have enjoyed my work, many more have never heard of it, a few have savaged it mercilessly. The point I want to make is that whatever happens, good or bad, your attitude is your professionalism and your professionalism is the platform on which you build your career. You make yourself a victim of other people's opinions just as much if you swagger over a good review as if you wilt under a bad one. We are just travellers on the road. All the advice in the world should not deter you from walking the way you want to go. Consider guidance carefully, but always decide for yourself.

Many, many times I've heard writers talk almost with pride about 'papering the walls with rejection slips' as though that were part of the apprenticeship. Well, maybe it is but it can still hurt if you don't actively prepare for it. Publishing, alas, is just another part of the cold hard machine of big business. If you are not marketable you will not be taken on.

However, before you ever get to the heady pinnacle of actually receiving a rejection slip, prepare yourself for the crushing inertia and apathy you will meet in the publishing world. On numerous occasions my books have sat for months (up to six months actually, see page 138) on the slush pile table, only to be returned unread. I know they were unread because of their pristine condition. Besides that, the sprinkle of talcum powder I put on page 3 had not been disturbed. I have also had editors' letters displaying a monumental ignorance about what I was trying to achieve, dismissed sometimes with those vacuous words 'It's not quite for us.'

Be ready too for those editors who think they can write your books better than you can. I once submitted a children's book for an educational series, only to have it returned covered in editorial notes - there were more words of correction on the manuscript than there were words of text. In her accompanying letter the editor hoped that her comments would be of some use. Well no, actually they weren't, not to me anyway. She was trying to turn my story into her story. Attempting to rewrite it according to her blueprint would have doomed it to failure, I'm sure.

Look out also for what I call the illusion of wisdom, which creates the impression that an editor knows something you don't, and that if only you *had* known it your book might have been accepted. Too late by then, of course. For instance, an editor once returned a manuscript explaining that they, the publishers, weren't going to accept it because 'it was only 87% of the way there.' I looked for the sheet clarifying what the missing 13% might be, but alas the editor must have forgotten to slip it into the envelope. On another occasion a returned manuscript was accompanied by the cryptic and tantalising message that the book was being rejected because 'it didn't have that certain something.' I wrote back asking what the certain something was, but I never got a reply (even though I included an SAE).

Then there are the editors who simply don't like what you've sent. That's fair enough, and at least it's honest. More irritating are the editors who don't like the *kind* of books you're writing. My Ben

Leech Horror novels were part of (as far as I could see) a flourishing list at a certain major publisher. However, after my third book came out my editor was made redundant and his replacement (yes, I know that makes no sense) declined my further submissions because he 'didn't like Horror.' I featured him anonymously in a subsequent horror story and he died most agonisingly, I assure you.

Might I also suggest that while film starlets might sleep with directors, you should not mix business with pleasure and get too friendly with your editor. It so happened that I once taught the son of a freelance editor who had been commissioned to develop a series of educational plays. This man was a fellow teacher and we'd gone out for drinks a few times. He was all set to take a couple of my plays when a parents' evening came along during which the gentleman felt that I wasn't pushing his son hard enough. Even though the boy was in the top set, I wasn't stretching him sufficiently. I asked how I could push and stretch his son at the same time. My plays were never published, nor indeed returned despite my polite letters (with SAE included).

Finally, so that I can feel I've earned my Grumpy Old Man medal, let me mention the time when I dared to complain to an editor who wanted to change the basic structure of an educational book I'd written less than a fortnight before the deadline. When I pointed out that incorporating her thoughts would virtually mean rewriting the whole thing, and that I didn't think her ideas really added much to the book, she invoked a clause in the contract and demanded her advance back! To add insult to injury, my agent - who had by this time deducted her 10% - refused to return her commission because she had 'worked hard on the contract.' I pointed out that I had worked hard on the book, but that didn't seem to influence her decision. I ended up paying back the agent's fee out of my own pocket and I parted company with her not long afterwards.

So, will this kind of thing happen to you? Almost certainly before, during and after you find success in your writing career. But however bad it gets, just remember that editors also are only human - although some of them don't have that certain something.

45

Vanity, Thy Name is Publishing!

> If I keep a green bough in my heart,
> the singing bird will come.
> *Chinese Proverb*

I wonder if there are any authors who are content to sit and write their stories without any wish to see them published? Even if I knew I'd never have another book accepted, I'd still write for as long as I was able to. (One of my literary heroes is H. G. Wells, who was writing on the last day of his life at age 80). But even so, I'd hate to think I'd have no chance of seeing my books in print ever again.

Which brings me on to self-publishing. I'm sure I don't need to labour the vital distinction between that and vanity publishing. Vanity publishers are little more than printers who, for a large profit, produce copies of your book and send them to you in boxes. You're left with the problem of storage, distribution and marketing. To some extent that's true if you self publish, but in this case you have much more control over the process and can ensure that you're not being ripped off. Self-publishing necessitates a name designated by the author as his publishing house appearing on the book's copyright page as publisher. Furthermore, the book's ISBN number must be registered with the ISBN Agency to that author as publisher, and all copies of the book are the property of the author to dispose of as he wishes.

I belong to the Society of Authors, who some years ago organised a seminar on self-publishing. To belong to the society you must have had at least two books published by a recognised publishing house.

When I received the leaflet advertising the seminar I decided to go, thinking that I'd be one of half a dozen sad failures whose books were being enthusiastically rejected by the big publishers (and the little ones, come to that). I was therefore astonished to find that over *two hundred* other authors had turned up, all of them dissatisfied for many different reasons with the mainstream world of publishing, all of them interested in having more say over their publishing careers.

My visit to that seminar coincided (uncannily) with my meeting a fellow writer named Peter Hayden. Peter writes children's books. His first title had been taken by a well-known publishing house, but Peter felt that both the production and promotion of the book were poor. The title was quickly remaindered, so Peter bought up the remaining stock and decided to sell the copies himself. He also vowed that from then on he would self-publish his work.

Because he visits many schools, Peter finds a ready market for his books. Some of his titles have sold so well that they have gone into a third printing, with a print run of a thousand copies or more. His enterprise has been so successful that he now publishes under the banner of Crazy Horse Press. He oversees all aspects of the production of his titles, as well as organising the printing and distribution of publicity leaflets. Peter tells me that the satisfaction he gets from self-publishing is immense.

As you may surmise, I'm a staunch advocate of the idea. You will quite rightly recognise that Peter Hayden is fortunate in being a sought-after visitor to schools, which offer a ready market for his work. That doesn't detract from his achievement, of course, but why would you want to spend hundreds or thousands of pounds for boxes of books gathering dust under the bed, apart from the few copies you gave away or managed to sell to friends?

The answer is that you don't need to. Some printing companies now offer print-on-demand, where you can order as few or as many copies of a title as you like *and pay per copy*. So if I wanted, say, fifty copies of a children's book to sell in schools, a print-on-demand company would produce that many and charge me a few pounds per copy. At that price I can afford to sell at a modest profit and the kids are still getting good value. When my fifty books are gone I can order a further fifty, and so on.

You will of course need to find an artist to create the front cover, although you might use a photograph. Digital cameras take high-resolution pictures that can be loaded straight into your computer for enhancement and straight into the printer's computer when the time comes to publish.

When the book is published you can sell copies online through a company like Amazon or, of course, you can offer direct to the public through your website - but in all cases do find out about your tax liability, as any books you sell count as income.

In any case investing in a few dozen self-published copies of your book would make a great showcase for your work, even if you didn't sell a single one. Take a few to your local library and ask if they could be put on the shelves. You might also splash out on a publicity poster - or create one for very little cost on the computer. Send review copies of the book to local newspapers and radio stations (Target a suitable programme and find out the name of the producer). If your book is suitable for a younger audience, make a gift of a copy or two to local schools. There is also nothing stopping you from taking copies to a high street bookstore, which might agree to give a local author a chance. But be prepared for the very high discount they'll want. Fifty percent is not unusual.

Making this effort might launch your career. Word of mouth is powerful and can pay dividends. A number of now well-known writers started out by self publishing their first books; word spread, they got noticed and publishing deals with major houses followed. The chances of this happening to you (or me) are not high, but if you don't try it, your chances are smaller even than that.

So, What's Your Attitude?

I hope that by now you feel that I've explored The Attitude thoroughly. In considering my or anyone else's opinions take an eclectic approach - use what works for you and make it your own. When all's said and done, and despite quite enjoying wearing my grumpy old man hat, I'm endlessly optimistic about my writing despite inevitable knocks. Over the years I have found the following thoughts sustaining.

* Everything that happens is useful material for writing.
* All criticism is only someone's opinion.
* Reviewing the reasons for writing nourishes a basic sense of purpose.
* Practice makes better. Nothing is perfect. Reviewing old work and realising its faults means you've moved on. Looking back is also looking forwards.
* When you are pleased with what you've done, thank yourself. I have long believed that talking to yourself in this way is the first sign of sanity (and paying attention is the second).
* Never throw any of your writing away (see point 1).
* Write your way out of any difficulty that is to do with your writing.
* Good judgement comes from experience and experience comes from bad judgement
* Your achievement comes in putting one word in front of another and repeating that process throughout your life.

47

Wishes and Goals, Pledges and Dares

> Thoughts rule the world.
> *Ralph Waldo Emerson*

My first published book was a story for children about how a little boy who was wishing his life away suddenly realised that his wishes were coming true - but never in the way he wanted them to, no matter how carefully he tried to frame the wish. The point of the story for me is that wishing wastes time and makes you the victim of inertia. Whenever I find wishful thinking creeping up on me I 'flip the coin' in my head and consider *active thinking*, which:

* Is under the individual's control.
* Involves a clear a sense of direction and destination.
* Requires planning and review at each stage.
* Flourishes in the presence of excitement and curiosity.
* Recognizes strategies as processes focussed on fixed goals.
* Expands and diversifies, exploiting all available resources.
* Remains rational (amenable to reason) and realistic, even while using what may appear to be irrational subconscious abilities and fantasy as a metaphor within the thinking arena.
* Supports and is supported by self belief, is strengthened by commitment and driven by joy.

48

The Road to Mastery

> The debt we owe to the play of the imagination is incalculable.
> *Carl Jung*

My work in education often brings me into contact with the notion of the 'learning curve' and some time ago I began wondering why it's a curve. The only answer I can think of is that it must have something to do with a curved line on a graph. But is that really how we learn, in a smooth upward sweep? In any case, it's not a helpful image to me as I imagine myself trying to scramble up that curve or at worst sliding back down a slippery slope!

I much prefer the metaphor of 'walking along the road to mastery.' This conjures images of a journey with scenery on the way, with ups and downs, interesting diversions, fascinating byways, unexpected vistas and, most of all, the whole world to explore. For me this is not a fanciful notion. If we are intent on being writers we need to have an overview in our heads of what our career might look like and involve. Such an overarching idea should be functional on the small scale too. If I'm on the road to mastery, therefore, do I have setbacks? No, I never turn around and go back towards the start. Whatever happens is 'local' to this stretch of the road and does not affect my intention to keep walking. Every step is an achievement. Every delay is followed by more steps forward. If I encounter a 'block' there is always a way around it, and even the largest block does not detract too much from the scenery and my appreciation of the landscape. Do I imagine myself competing with fellow travellers? No, this is not a race to be won. Let others run as fast as they like. I'll go at a pace that suits me.

Finally, does practice make perfect? No, at best practice makes better. It's the journey that counts - does a destination even exist? I do bear in mind though, having been writing for thirty-five years, that I want thirty-five years' worth of experience, and not one year's worth of experience thirty-five times. As I journey I think about the journey; what I've seen, where I'm going, what's around me now. In doing so, I never lose my way. . .

So that's a metaphor which works for me. What might work best for you?

49

50 Ideas to Boost Your Writing

Every Day Parables

> Out of clutter, find simplicity.
> From discord, find harmony.
> In the middle of difficulty, find opportunity.
> *Albert Einstein*

Although I've dismissed writer's block as a figment of the imagination, I don't disdain it or underestimate the feeling of frustration or panic when the words won't come. And while I can put on my grumpy act when it comes to editors I don't agree with, or publishing companies who ignore me, or critics who don't like my work, these people's comments can still hurt. A story or poem has been described as someone's heart in another person's hands, and we can all bruise easily. Our vulnerability is not to be denied, but neither should fear or hurt prevent us from journeying onward.

I have found that writing short parables to myself, about myself, has helped me often to overcome difficult situations. Such little tales are a creative challenge and very enjoyable to do. They also help me to have a sense of perspective on events that might otherwise crush or defeat me. If you use this idea yourself, then you can 'translate' existing traditional tales to suit your purposes, or of course make up the stories from scratch. Here are a couple of examples.

The Backwards-Walking Traveller

A little way along the path, a brother and sister saw a most curious sight. Coming towards them was a man, who appeared to be carrying a sack of stones upon his back. He was walking with great determination, almost with anger, and certainly with much grunting and groaning, for the stones were obviously very heavy and a huge burden to him. But stranger still, he was striding backwards, his gaze fixed intently upon the path he had already walked.

After a few moments, the man stopped, bent down, picked up yet another rock and dropped it into his bag, which he then shouldered before carrying on.

"Look out!" yelled the sister, as she spotted the man coming up to a hole in the ground. He seemed not to hear her, and the next second he dropped into the opening with a crash and a clatter.

He clambered out, muttering and swearing, his anger intensified; grabbed yet another handful of stones and placed them in his sack before resuming his backwards march.

"Excuse me sir," said the brother politely. "But why do you carry that sack of rocks on your shoulders?"

"They remind me of things," he replied promptly. "Look, I'll show you."

Without slowing down, he plucked out a stone and glared at it as he spoke. "This one is rage for all the times people have been unfair to me."

He tossed it back in the sack and snatched another. "And this one is failure... And this, missed opportunities... And this one is youth which has gone forever. It looks small and hardly any weight at all, but I can tell you it's the hardest one of all to bear..."

"Can I ask, sir," said the sister, "why you are walking backwards like this?"

"I can't get the past out of my sight, child," the man told her. "Because all of these stones never cease to remind me of it."

"Doesn't there seem to be an obvious solution to this problem?" the brother said.

The man shrugged. "Why yes. I try not to let it get me down. And whenever I fall into a hole, I jump back up, dust myself off, and start all over again! Now excuse me, I have much to do..."

And the children stared after him as the man paused to pick up another stone, and strode off backwards into the future.

The Ladybirds

One day Susan was out by herself in the garden. The morning had been wet and thundery, but now the sun was shining warmly down on her as she explored, noticing all kinds of small things for the first time.

After a few minutes of wandering thus, she came across two ladybirds on a leaf. They were engaged in what looked to be a fierce struggle, locked together in combat as they rolled this way and that. Both ladybirds were startlingly different from anything Susan had seen before. One was pure white, yet had a single black spot in the middle of its back. The other was pure black, and in the centre of its back was a solitary white dot.

Susan liked the look of the white ladybird: it seemed clean and nice, and kind of sunny like the afternoon had turned out. On the other hand, the appearance of the black ladybird frightened her rather: it looked sinister, menacing and evil.

The child watched as a subtle balance tipped and the black ladybird rolled on top of its white opponent. Then, after some seconds of effort, the tables were turned and the white ladybird managed to gain the advantage. But then the black enemy, with a renewed effort, regained its ascendancy...

Susan decided she had better do something about this, before the white ladybird was harmed or killed.

She reached out to separate the two insects, but found they could not be moved. No matter how hard she tried, she was unable to draw the ladybirds apart, so closely and tightly were they intertwined.

She became so engrossed in her mission that for some minutes she failed to notice the black clouds piling up in the sky, until a rumble of thunder alerted her.

Susan gazed up, apprehensive at first, then relieved to see that the storm was coming to nothing, the clouds sliding away to let the sun once more shine brilliantly down.

And then, understanding, she let the ladybirds go, because the force that bound them was no different to that which made the day and the night, summer and winter, life and death, the stars and the spaces between them.

50

CREATE

50 Ideas to Boost Your Writing

> You cannot tread the path
> until you have become that path yourself.
> *Traditional saying*

Mahatma Gandhi was once asked what his message was. He replied, 'I am the message.' By the same token, writing is not simply something we do, it is something we are. We don't just have an attitude towards the craft; the attitude is built into our bones. Each of us has a past that is rich in experience, a future that is full of potential and a present moment pregnant with opportunity. So let's use the present moment to CREATE.

Connect Relate Explore Analyse Transform Experience

And in doing so remember . . .

I am the wizard!
Inside me float the moon and stars -
They shine as brightly as I
Make them shine.

Here within me are the seas and skies,
The fields and forests and mountains -
All of these - all! - are mine.

Somewhere nearby there lies tomorrow
Like a misty road.
Where does it go?
Anywhere I make it so.

And should I run or wander slow
It's still a road,
And by the way the grass all by itself will grow.

In my domain I am the Queen and King
And all the common kin.
And when they quarrel
So I quarrel
And where they sin
I sin.

All their yesterdays
Is my time too.
I end with them
And with them must I start.

And here at the core of our kingdom
Lies our greatest precious treasure -
Now! - this moment - Now!
Measured out and made alive
By the beating of my heart.

I am my own magic,
I weave my own bright spell.
And I have learned this trick -
I listen closely when I tell.

And wonder finds me
Wherever I may seek,
For I am the wizard -
Abracadabrah!
I create life as I speak.

Index

Active Thinking - 152
Agents - 143
Anchoring Behaviours - 27, 84
Artful Vagueness - 14, 60, 96
Attitude to Writing - 9, 116, 151, 155
Audience - 121
Author Intrusion - 76
Because Game (logical thinking) - 45
Bifurcations (alternative scenarios) - 105
Blurbs - 112
Characters - 49
- depth in - 56, 62
- and emotions - 84
- naming - 54
- 'types' - 53
Chronology - 47
Contexts - 45
Diaries - 102
Disney Strategy (for developing ideas) - 109
Editors - 123, 141
Elements of Narrative - 15
Emotions - 28, 83, 126
Empathy - 17
Everyday Parables (as teachings) - 155
Going Along for the Ride (short story for review) - 130
Fortunately-Unfortunately Game (and point of view) - 102
Genre - 42
Hill, Douglas (prolific Fantasy and Science Fiction writer) - 10, 26, 78, 104
I am the Wizard (a poem with attitude) - 159

Ideas - 11
Imagination - 27
Ingredients (flavouring a story) - 42
Inspiration - 71, 121
Instress and Inscape (uniqueness in things) - 71
Intention (as an aspect of the creative attitude) - 9, 13, 25
I Wonder Game (speculation) - 18
Mastering the craft - 153
Merlin Game (brainstorming) - 100
Metaphorical Thinking - 59
'Mood' for writing - see Anchoring Behaviours
Motifs - 43, 94
Multi-sensory Description - 35
Naming Characters - 54
Nerve, failure of - 9
Nonsense Words - 86
Observing - 34
Perceptions - 28
Perspectives - 17, 75
PIN Technique (Positive-Interesting-Negative) - 60
Plagiarism - 108
Print-on-demand (and self publishing) - 147
Propp, Valdimir (folklorist) - 15
Pseudonyms - 113
Publishing, self- and vanity- - 147
Questions, six big important - 30
Reviewing your work - 31, 109, 118 125
Seed Thoughts (ideas in potential) - 26
Settings - 70
- fictitious - 78
Sleeping on ideas - 24

Something Goes By
           (nonsense poem) - 89
Stereotypes - 53, 62
Storylines - 21, 30, 40, 96
Story Tree - 106
Stream-of-Consciousness
           writing - 104
Style - 128
Subconscious - 11, 21
Submitting work - 138

Synaesthesia (mixing the
           senses) - 80
Ten Sentence Game - 98
Themes - 38
Visualising - 36, 66
Vivid Particularities (vivid images
        with emotional impact) - 52
While Game - see Contexts
Wishful Thinking - 152
Writer's Block - 9, 84, 100
Zig-Zag Story Game - 147

Illustrations:

Fig.1: Image Grid - 12
Fig.2: Family? - 18
Fig.3: Story Line - 22
Fig.4: The Mirror - 32
Fig.5: Bottom-Up Town-Down
           Pyramid - 39
Fig.6: Sub-Elements Grid - 41
Fig.7: Character Pyramid - 57

Fig.8: A Bundle of
           Contradictions - 63
Fig.9: Cross-match Characters - 67
Fig.10: The World Inside - 68
Fig.11: Kitiki and Boobah - 87
Fig.12: The Walker - 92
Fig.13: Fortune Cookie
           Language - 97